BURNLEY FC

MISCELLANY

BURNLEY FC

MISCELLANY

DAVID CLAYTON

AMBERLEY

For a man who enjoys a drop of Clarets, Chris Eccles, and to the memory of Burnley FC apprentice Ben Lee

First published 2014

Amberley Publishing
The Hill, Stroud
Gloucestershire, GL5 4EP

www.amberley-books.com

British Library Cataloguing in Publication Data.
A catalogue record for this book is available from the British Library.

ISBN 978 1 4456 4223 9 (print)
ISBN 978 1 4456 4245 1 (ebook)

Typesetting and Origination by Amberley Publishing.
Printed in the UK.

CONTENTS

ACKNOWLEDGEMENTS

Thanks to my mate, Chris Eccles, for sharing his Clarets treasure trove with me during my research for this book. To all the guys who run 'Clarets Mad', and big thanks for the wealth of infomation contained within your site – it was more than useful for cross-checking, and led to a number of new avenues and is the best site I came across while researching this book, so a massive thanks guys. The Longside Reference and Clarets organisation also came in very handy to check, and occasionally inspire, along the way too.

Thanks to the countless journalists, programme editors and supporters who committed their thoughts to print over the years, and everyone who has unknowingly played a part in the creation of this book – too many to thank personally, but I thank you all nonetheless.

One thing I didn't do was consult Dave Wiseman's *Burnley Miscellany*. When I was asked to write this book, I decided that although the *Miscellany* would be the ideal place to find added inspiration when I needed it, it would have been too tempting to delve into often, and be lazy on my part. Hopefully, if you have both *Miscellany* books, that will be clear enough, though I'm sure we have covered a number of similar findings. If there's any justice, both mine and Dave's will be must-have purchases for any respectable Claret!

I've written a number of books on football clubs, but I really enjoyed researching the Clarets' history, and finding out so much about a team that lies so close to where I live. Burnley has always been what I call a 'proper club' – supported by generations of the same families; a core of support who have stuck with the club through thin, thinner and latterly thicker times. The average attendance against the local population also makes this club one of the best supported in the nation and, ah well, you already know all this.

Promotion back to the Premier League has given Burnley a real chance to not only rub shoulders with the great and good, but perhaps take a place among them on a more permanent basis – something that hasn't been the case for far too long. With such proud traditions, it's about time there was fresh blood at the top table, and the Clarets have earned the right to reclaim a spot that was, for so long, deservedly theirs.

It may be a big ask to repeat the successes of the 1960s, but as a famous sportswear giant likes to tell us, 'impossible is nothing'.

Finally, thanks to Tom Furby at Amberley Publishing for giving me the opportunity to write about Burnley Football Club, and also to my wife and three kids, who I had to sacrifice precious time with as the deadline loomed.

I hope you, the reader, enjoy the book and, even if it's saved for those precious quiet few minutes in the smallest room in the house, that's good enough for me.

BURNLEY FC

MISCELLANY

REBELS WITH A CAUSE

Burnley FC may have been one of the new boys on the block, but it didn't stop them fighting for their own corner. The issue was the Clarets felt some players should be paid for playing and the FA disagreed, wanting to keep association football strictly an amateur affair. The rift steadily grew ,with Burnley eventually heading a breakaway group intent on having their own league and rules if need be. In 1885, with their hand forced, the FA relaxed their rules to allow players to be paid.

It was a victory for common sense if football was to flourish, and it meant the clubs who could afford to, were able to enhance their squad and tempt better players on board to progress. The best players at Turf Moor were on a small fortune – £2 per week – and even the lesser lights were earning a decent wage, though much of the money came from club benefactor, Charles Massey, owner of a local brewery. Through a mixture of improving football, publicity and curiosity, the fans started to trickle in, and the club and Burnley FC was truly up and running.

In 1888, the Clarets became one of the founder members of the progressive Football League when they accepted an invitation to join other teams from the North West and the Midlands.

CULT HERO NO. I: GARY CAHILL

Gary Cahill arrived at Turf Moor in November 2004. Loaned from Aston Villa, initially on a month-long deal, the eighteen-year-old made an instant impression on his teammates and supporters, with a maturity that was well beyond his teenage years.

Cahill was so consistent during his spell. The deal was extended to a season-long loan, and the future England centre-half played thirty-two times and scored one goal during his time with the Clarets. He then picked up both the club's Young Player of the Year award and the Player of the Year award. His star was rising rapidly, and though boss Steve Cotterill would have loved to have made the deal permanent, the asking price was out of the Clarets' reach. He returned to Villa and though Cahill saw occasional first-team action for Villa, he failed to establish himself and was forced to seek another loan – this time with Sheffield United – before Bolton bought the twenty-two-year-old in 2008.

Before Cahill moved to Chelsea in 2012, he had become one of the hottest properties in English football – but he never forgot the part the Clarets played in his development. In an interview in 2012, he said,

Burnley are a club who gave me my first chance and built my career really, or started my career for me.

They gave me a chance and I took the chance. I've got very fond memories, it was brilliant. It was Steve Cotterill who took a chance on me. It took great bottle from him and I owe him a lot. I liked him and I got on well with him.

He brought my career on and I got thirty-odd games in which helped my career no end. Steve said to me when I got there that it was a 'sink or swim' scenario. Thankfully it went well for me there and I got on with everyone and the manager was brilliant. He played me every game I was fit.

THE MANAGERS
NO. 1: ARTHUR SUTCLIFFE, 1893–96

The Clarets began life with no manager as such for the first five years of existence – as did many fledgling football clubs – and it was very much a collective decision to pick the team and make decisions regarding players. The final League positions varied from eleventh to sixth during that period. As we all know, a camel is a horse designed by a committee, and too many opinions do not make a good decision. In 1893, it was decided that Arthur Sutcliffe could fill the role of team decisions while continuing his role as club secretary, and the new man at the helm immediately stamped his mark on the club, introducing a policy of unearthing local talent rather than rely on a constant source of players from Scotland. His policy soon paid dividends with the Clarets pushing for the title at one stage, turning Turf Moor into a fortress, winning thirteen of the fifteen games played at home during the 1893/94 campaign. Though they eventually slipped to fifth spot, this was the club's highest finish so far.

The second season was tougher, with star players, Jack Hillman and Pete Turnbull, both leaving for Everton and the Clarets, now fielding almost an entirely home-grown – and much younger – team. Subsequently, the team finished ninth, losing nine of the final ten games to slip from fifth.

The third and final campaign under Sutcliffe's tenure was the toughest, with virtually all of his best players moving on and a dreadful sequence of nine losses and three defeats early on in the season. Sutcliffe though had the wherewithal to steer the club out of the depths and finish with just two defeats in the final twelve matches. The high point was the final game of the season, Sutcliffe's last game in charge, where Blackburn Rovers were thrashed 6-0 ensuring a tenth place finish.

GIVE IT TO GORDON!

With more than 700 games under his belt, Gordon Cowans arrived at Turf Moor in 1997. The majority of his career had been in the claret and blue of Aston Villa, and he was thirty-nine when he took up the role as Burnley reserve team boss at the behest of manager Chris Waddle. However, an injury crisis meant Cowans, capped ten times by England, was forced to dust off his boots and play for the first team during the 1997/98 campaign. Under his tutelage, the Burnley second team would go on to win promotion, but his spell in the first team wasn't quite as profitable. He made his debut in a 2-0 Coca-Cola Cup defeat to Stoke City, and he played again three days later in a 2-1 loss to Brentford, before a five-week break and a final run of seven games in November, which saw the Clarets win two, draw once and lose four times. Seven games in twenty-four days were enough to convince Cowans never to play again, and he left at the end of the season to rejoin his first love, Aston Villa, where he has held the posts of first team coach, academy coach and assistant manager over the last sixteen years. His playing record is: Appearances 9, Goals 0.

GENTILE DOES IT...

Marco Gentile played just once for the Clarets – a 2-0 defeat to Stoke in 1997 – before moving on, having failed to impress. Gentile, a Dutch central defender who made a steady career for himself in Holland with Den Haag, returned to his homeland for three years before trying his luck in British football once again, this time with Dumbarton. He played just twice before once again returning to Holland, his ambitions unrealised.

ROCKIN' RONNIE

Ron Futcher was that rarest of beasts – a natural goal-scorer who had a decent record wherever he played. Twin of defender, Paul Futcher, Ron started out at Chester before making a name for himself at Luton Town. For the third time in his career, he followed his brother and joined Manchester City, and though things didn't quite work out, he still scored a hat-trick in one away game to Chelsea. He then spent time in the USA and was a prolific scorer for Minnesota Kicks, Portland Timbers and Tulsa Roughnecks, before returning to England with Barnsley, Oldham, Bradford and Port Vale – finishing top scorer for the latter three teams. He was snapped up by the Clarets for £60,000 in November 1989, even though he was thirty-three years old. Futcher repaid the investment by scoring ten goals and topping the scoring charts for Frank Casper's side, and his first full season saw him grab twenty goals in forty-three appearances. He moved on in 1991 to Crewe, and ended his career with Boston United. His stay at Turf Moor won him a number of admirers. However, many of them wondered how good he could have been, had he joined three or four seasons earlier.

THESE COLOURS DON'T RUN – BUT WE DON'T LIKE THEM!

As stated previously, the Clarets began life as anything but a club, and searched hard for its identity. Long before the decision to copy Aston Villa's kit, Burnley FC played in four different combinations of striped kit, then red shirts before donning a much-disliked green kit. They finally settled on claret and blue in 1910. Can you imagine 'come on you stripey greens?' Doesn't sound right, does it?

MASCOT GRAND NATIONAL

Alas, Bertie Bee has never troubled the winner's podium at the annual Mascot Grand National. First held at Huntingdon Racecourse in 1999, when seventeen mascots raced over 220 yards and six hurdles, Birmingham City's Beau Brummie Bear won the inaugural event. By 2000, numbers had swelled to forty-nine mascots, with Watford's Harry the Hornet taking the crown. There was controversy in 2001 when Freddie the Fox cantered home way ahead of everyone else – only to be unmasked as an Olympic athlete and disqualified! The race has since moved to Kempton, and though Bertie still awaits his moment in the sun, his cousin, Barnet's Mr Bumble, won the race in 2010 and 2012.

THE MANAGERS
NO. 2: HARRY BRADSHAW 1896–99

Harry Bradshaw was first secretary, and then chairman, of Burnley before succeeding Arthur Sutcliffe as manager in 1896. Bradshaw's tenure began in the worst possible fashion, as the Clarets lost ten and drew two of the final fourteen games and found themselves in a relegation test match series with Manchester United and then Notts County. A 2-1 aggregate defeat to the latter meant demotion for the Clarets to the second tier for the first time.

Bradshaw acted quickly and captured highly rated duo Wilf Toman and Jimmy Ross. The pair's goals saw the Clarets score just half of the eighty goals scored that season, to finish as champions and earn promotion via the test match method, which included two wins over Blackburn. The good form continued back into the top flight, with a record high finish of third place – the best in the club's eleven-year Football League existence. For Bradshaw, it was a fitting end to his time at Turf Moor, and he opted for a move south where he became Woolwich Arsenal manager.

SUMO, SUMO, SUMO!

Physiotherapist Andy Jones was given the unfortunate nickname Sumo, due to his chunky (being kind) physique, and the chant was invariably heard whenever Andy ran on to treat a player. He left in 1997 and later went to Sheffield United and Charlton Athletic with, no doubt, the unflattering chant following him wherever he went.

SKULDUGGERY AT THE MOOR

In January 2011, thieves broke into Turf Moor and stole a flag being flown at half-mast in respect of former Claret Ralph Coates, who had passed away two weeks before. The thieves were caught on CCTV around 2 a.m. on New Year's Day, walking behind the Bob Lord Stand before making off towards the city centre.

The flag measured 6 feet by 4 feet and had the club's crest and Latin phrase *pretiumque et causa laboris*, which means 'the prize is the cause of our labours' written on it. The culprits were never identified, nor were the vandals who cut loose a BFC blimp that was about to make its maiden voyage above Turf Moor.

FIVE-STAR ANDY

Most players never score a hat-trick in their professional career, and fewer still manage to find the net four times in one game – enter

Andy Lochead who managed the bang five goals in one game. Make that in two games! Yes, Andy achieved what is an incredible feat on two separate occasions. The first was when the Clarets thumped Chelsea 6-2 at Turf Moor during the 1964/65 campaign, and then, the following season, he did it again, scoring five goals in a 7-0 FA Cup third round replay victory over Bournemouth at Turf Moor. Andy's scoring exploits are likely never to be repeated and in 226 games, the big Scot bagged 101 goals during an eight-year period in East Lancashire.

PLAY THE WILD ROVER

In one of those 'it could only happen to us' games, the Clarets took on FA Cup holders Blackburn Rovers at Turf Moor in atrocious conditions of driving snow and blizzards. Tough Burnley adapted better to the wintry blast by establishing a 3-0 lead by the break.

It was 12 December 1891, and Rovers at least knew that they would have a strong wind behind them after the break and an opportunity to get back in the game. Yet, either because they were too cold or perhaps in protest, only seven Rovers players emerged for the second half, but soon they were down to six when the visitors' Joe Lofthouse clashed with Clarets' star Alex Stewart, and both were sent for an early bath. Perhaps sensing an opportunity, the remaining Blackburn players then walked off the pitch, leaving only their goalkeeper on the Turf Moor pitch. The Clarets played on and, during their next attack, scored a goal. The referee ruled the goal out for offside, and promptly abandoned proceedings, but there was some justice and common sense in the decision to allow the result to stand.

CURSED KIT?

The half green and black away shirts the Clarets wore during the 1993/94 campaign were undoubtedly jinxed, and the first time they were used resulted in a 4-1 defeat to Rochdale. Burley failed to win a League game with the shirt on, and only managed a draw on one occasion. Their only success was a 3-2 FA Cup win at York when the Clarets had a man sent off. The kit was ditched for the 1994/95 campaign, but it would have the last laugh when Southend visited Turf Moor on 31 December 1994. The Shrimpers' shirts clashed with Burnley's and they were offered the green and black strip from the season before as an alternative. The Clarets, perhaps sensing closure on the whole affair, went on to thrash Southend 5-1. The kit was never seen again...

IN THE BEGINNING

The Burnley FC we know today was originally formed as a rugby union club called Burnley Rovers in the 1870s.

Football was growing in popularity and a number of clubs formed in the town. On 18 May 1882, a meeting was held in the Bull Hotel on Manchester Road and it was agreed to leave the oval shaped ball behind and become a football club. At the same meeting, they also dropped Rovers from the fledgling club's name.

With facilities at Burnley's former Calder Vale home perhaps better suited to rugby, Burnley Cricket Club offered their sporting neighbours the opportunity to share their Turf Moor sports field – once no more than a large grassy field and a coal pit during the heady days of the Industrial Revolution. In September 1883, Burnley FC had a new home, after they'd stumped up the princely sum of £65 to move. It was a ground that would still be home some 131 years later, and only Lancastrian neighbours Preston North End have played longer in a stadium.

THE 3.33 FROM TURF MOOR

In January 1996, Burnley fans decided to protest against chairman Frank Teasdale's regime by turning their backs on the game at a proposed time. So during the home clash against Crewe, at 3.33 p.m., thousands of supporters did exactly that and turned their backs on the game as a show of displeasure of Teasdale's reign. The chairman's response though was to sack manager Jimmy Mullen after the game with the Railwaymen. Teasdale continued his chairmanship for another two years, after which supporters organised a sit-in after the game with Notts County at Turf Moor. The result of the protest was the introduction of local businessman Barry Kilby, who became chairman two months later, remaining in the position until 2012, when he was forced to step down due to ill health.

HAIRCUT, SIR?

Rumours that the Clarets signing Tony Morley incurred the wrath of chairman, Bob Lord, are probably true. Morley, a winger captured from Preston North End for £100,000, arrived at Turf Moor with flowing blond locks and was 'advised' by Lord to get his hair cut. Apparently, he turned up with a shaven head not long after, which backfired as it revealed his earring that Lord disliked even more. Despite the fashion clashes, Morley remained at Turf Moor for three seasons, before swapping claret and blue for, erm, claret and blue as he signed for Aston Villa in 1979 for £200,000.

NOBLE GESTURE

Burnley legend Peter Noble left his mark on the game in more than one way during an esteemed career with Newcastle, Swindon, the Clarets and Blackpool, all of whom he served with great distinction. Among his notable achievements, he scored the winning goal for Swindon against Burnley in the 1969 League Cup semi-final and played in the final against Arsenal where the Third Division Robins caused one of the greatest upsets of all-time, winning 3-1 against the Gunners. He also played against Fabio Capello during an Anglo-Italian Cup tie against Roma – a game that confirmed Capello's admiration of the English game and perhaps influenced him to become England manager in later years. A committed and whole-hearted player, Burnley paid £40,000 for Nobel's services, and he repaid that in full over a seven-year period, playing 248 games and scoring sixty-three goals, but it was his record of scoring all twenty-eight penalties that he took that earned him a place in the board game Trivial Pursuit.

THEY SAID IT...

Owen Coyle reacts, after the Clarets hold Manchester City to a 3-3 draw at the Etihad in November 2009:

> We are on a learning curve and if we had been an experienced Premier League team we would have seen it off. There is an unbelievable spirit in our dressing room. We are the smallest town to be in the Premier League, but we are determined to give this a real fight. Getting into the Premier League was an unbelievable achievement, but staying in it would exceed that by some distance.

Brian Jensen, creating a problem for himself in 2009:

After the Chelsea game I went into Harrods, I was only waiting for the team bus to arrive but, because I decided to buy the missus a pair of shoes and had to ring her up because I didn't know her shoe size, the Danish press built it up into some kind of footballers' wives thing. And now she wants another pair after the Arsenal game. It's a shambles.

Burnley's irrepressible former chairman Bob Lord airs his displeasure at increased TV coverage:

If the BBC don't shift their cameras from Turf Moor I'll be down there myself and personally burn them. They are on the ground without our consent and I don't care if even Harold Wilson (then Prime Minister) has given them permission.

Chairman Bob Lord – what he said went during his reign at Turf Moor:

We are not having an official supporters' club at Burnley. They cause a lot of problems because the people who run them eventually want the football club power.

COUNTDOWN IS COMMENCING...

Clarke Carlisle, we can safely say, is the only former Burnley player to have appeared – and won – on Channel 4's legendary TV quiz shows *Countdown* and *Question Time*. In September 2013, he told the *Yorkshire Evening Post* that these were four of his favourite things:

TEAMMATE: Aaron Lennon at Leeds. His acceleration was just awesome.
OPPONENT: Didier Drogba, he has every attribute a striker needs.
MANAGER: Aidy Boothroyd. Meticulous, great knowledge of the game.
MOMENT: Winning the play-off final with Burnley to get to the Premier League.

THE MANAGERS
NO. 3: ERNEST MANGNALL 1899–1903

Burnley didn't have to look far for a manager to replace Harry Bradshaw. Bolton boss Ernest Mangnall took over at Turf Moor to guide the Clarets into the twentieth century. Mangnall inherited an ageing side and things couldn't have begun worse, as the team that had finished third the previous season were relegated on the final day after a 4-0 defeat at Nottingham Forest. To rub salt in the wounds, Mangnall saw his former employers, Bolton, replace the Clarets in the top flight!

For much of Mangnall's second season in charge, the Clarets looked a certainty for promotion, with a magnificent run of ten wins from eleven games taking the club to the top. But just two wins in the last ten games saw Birmingham and Grimsby edge ahead, and another season in Division Two was confirmed. Mangnall's reign only got worse with a ninth place finish in 1901/02, topped off with the Clarets finishing bottom of the entire Football League in 1902/03 and having to apply for re-election, which, thankfully, was successfully sought. For Mangnall, however, his fairly disastrous time at Turf Moor was at an end, but far from disappearing off the radar, he would go on to manage both Manchester United and Manchester City over the next twenty years, winning the First Division title for each Manchester side in the process!

FLEDGLING CLARETS

Several top players began life at Burnley and went on to enjoy great success in their career elsewhere – or at least enjoyed a brief spell. Lee Dixon came through the club's youth system and played four games before moving to Chester for a season. He then spent a year with

Bury, before earning his first prominent move to Stoke City. After two years at the Potteries, he joined Arsenal and he went on to play more than 500 games for the Gunners over a fourteen-year period.

Mike Phelan came through the youth system at Turf Moor as well, spending six years with the Clarets before moving to Norwich City and later Manchester United, where he would eventually become Sir Alex Ferguson's assistant manager. Trevor Steven came through the ranks and played more than seventy games for Burnley between 1980 and 1983, before moving to Everton where he won the majority of his thirty-six England caps.

In recent years, Kyle Laffetry and Jay Rodriguez both spent several years at Turf Moor, before moving on to big money deals with Rangers and Southampton respectively.

OFF AND RUNNING...

Burnley's first game at Turf Moor was against humble opposition – a local club recorded as 'Rowtenstall', but this was surely Rawtenstall? Either way, the visitors left with a 6-3 win, forever writing their name into the history books. On a sloping pitch that would take almost 100 years to put right, a handful of hardy souls gathered on a small hillock that afforded a decent view of what was no more than a large field at the time. So it was an auspicious start – 'Of such inconsequential beginnings, dynasties are begun', Stephen King once wrote. How true.

CULT HERO NO. 2: GEORGE OGHANI

Some players, often journeymen, have a couple of seasons where they really shine and show a glimpse of what might have been – George Oghani very much fits the bill for Burnley.

Signed in 1987 by boss Brian Miller, Oghani had made a name for himself in non-league football with Hyde United before finally getting a break with Bolton Wanderers.

He arrived at Turf Moor along with several other players and hit the ground running, scoring twenty goals in his first season, one of those being a superb strike in the Sherpa Van Trophy Northern Final against Preston North End. By the end of the season he was a firm favourite with Clarets fans.

Things didn't go so well for Oghani in his second season, and he had one or two off-the-field problems that seemed to affect his form and, after a training ground incident in April 1989, he was sold to Stockport County.

He bagged twenty-seven goals in ninety-three games and would go on to play for another eight teams before finally hanging his boots up. There were some highpoints in the days after Turf Moor, but few would argue with Oghani's first season in claret as perhaps the best of his career.

REJECTED BY CLARETS

Some illustrious names have slipped through the Clarets' net over the years. Future England and Manchester United captain Bryan Robson was told he was too small to make it as a footballer, and Ian Rush was also deemed not good enough to make the cut, before eventually going on to become Liverpool's record scorer. Lee Dixon was released as a teenager by manager John Bond. Andreas Villas Boas could have ended up as manager at Turf Moor as well, as former chief executive Paul Fletcher revealed in his 2012 autobiography, *Magical: A Life In Football.*

> Mickey Walsh, an old playing colleague of mine, got in touch with me to describe Andre as being a real up and coming hot prospect.
>
> He sent a very detailed and lengthy application for the job. His CV and Powerpoint presentation were amazing. Even by today's standards

there was some complicated stuff in it, with some things that I didn't understand.

Tommy Docherty used to say he never said anything to his players his milkman wouldn't understand. I don't think any milkman would fathom the meaning of a lot of Andre's presentation.

The language and jargon of football gets worse by the day. Villas-Boas uses a lot of it. Would Burnley players have ever understood what he wanted if he'd told them to 'solidificate' or some of his other terms?

Probably not! Finally, Stan Ternent played just five games between 1966 and 1968 before his unspectacular playing career move on to Carlisle United, but he came back, of course.

ALL FOUR ONE, FOUR FOR ALL

The Clarets have been involved in 4-4 draws on three separate occasions, all of which have been at Turf Moor. In March 1961, Burnley drew 4-4 with Chelsea and in 1975, Norwich also left East Lancashire having shared eight goals. The final 4-4 was just a year later with the Clarets drawing with Charlton Athletic.

THE MANAGERS
NO. 4: SPEN WHITTAKER 1903–10

Spen Whittaker would become the Clarets' first dedicated team manager when he succeeded Ernest Mangnall in 1903. For Whittaker, who arrived from Accrington, the only way was up, and he set about steadily rebuilding the team with a number of solid signings, including Hugh Moffatt. The first season under the new manager reflected his measured approach with a decent fifth-place finish. Though he introduced a number of excellent players, the signing of goalkeeper and former blacksmith, Jerry Dawson, was perhaps the best. Dawson eventually went on to become the Clarets' record-appearance holder, over more than a decade of service for the club.

But Whittaker couldn't guide the club back to the promised land, and the Clarets became used to mid-table finishes with eleventh, ninth and successive seventh place finishes in the next four seasons. Spen's final two campaigns ended even more disappointingly, with fourteenth place the final position in successive campaigns. Despite the lack of success, the board kept faith in their manager and he was allowed to start another rebuilding project. Harry Swift was signed from Accrington, and Spen headed off to London by train to register his papers in April 1910, but then tragedy struck. As his train arrived at Crewe, reports that a person had fallen from the moving train led to a search along the line whereby the body of Spen Whittaker was discovered. How the accident happened will never be known, but the club went into mourning when the news filtered back to Turf Moor, and a testimonial was soon arranged for Spen's family with a game against Manchester United.

ARE WE CITY IN DISGUISE?

Did Burnley wear sky-blue and white long before Lancastrian neighbours Manchester City did? Some of the earliest reports of Burnley's games suggest the club played in pale-blue and white – and even had a green kit for several years. In fact, it wouldn't be until 1910 that Burnley decided to pay homage to one of the powerhouses of the day thanks, to the progressive thinking of manager John Haworth. Aston Villa were worthy of imitation and so, wisely, the club hierarchy deigned fit to switch to claret and blue. It was thought a colour switch might inspire success similar to Villa's, and Burnley acquired a new nickname 'the Clarets'. About time, too. It didn't, however, inspire promotion during the first season in the new colours, with Burnley finishing eighth in Division Two, but at least Turf Moor became something of a fortress with just one defeat in nineteen games. The season after was even better, with fourteen wins and five draws, helping the Clarets to third place and just two points off winning the title. It also meant that the club had suffered just one defeat in thirty-eight home games since switching colours. Finally, just two losses in nineteen Turf Moor games saw a second-place finish in 1912/13, and a record of just three losses in fifty-seven matches. We'll end it there, but let's just say it was a good move.

THE BATTLE OF BRITAIN

Burnley and Celtic have had a few feisty meetings down the years, and the rivalry can be traced back more than 100 years. In May 1914, the Clarets and Celtic met in Budapest to raise money for Balkan war refugees. Describing it, the *Glasgow Herald* match report of 22 May simply states, 'Celtic, 1; Burnley, 1. At Budapest. The game was very rough, and exciting scenes took place at the finish. The competition cup was withheld.' Twenty-four words from Glasgow's main newspaper for a local team, whereas the *Burnley Express* gave a comprehensive report and summary.

> It was arranged that Celtic and Burnley would clash at the FTC Stadion, home of Ferencvaros, for the prize of a handsome silver cup – in the shape of a lighthouse – donated by local newspaper the *Hungarian News*. The hosts had failed to mention this game to Celtic, but once in the city the club altered its tour schedule to take part.

Ironically this match was dubbed a 'Battle of Britain', and then Great Britain and Ireland were at war with Austria, Germany and Hungary only a short time later. 21 May was a hot day in Budapest, and the two sides met on a dry and bumpy pitch before a crowd of around 10,000.

The match was a hard and ill-tempered contest. Jimmy McMenemy put Celtic in front through a twentieth-minute penalty. Burnley equalised from the penalty mark in the second half when Sunny Jim Young handled. Contemporary reports suggest that Celtic declined to play extra time. They agreed to travel to Burnley at a later date for a replay, and the Hungarians were to forward the trophy.

SELECTED TESTIMONIALS

There have been numerous testimonials down the years, some well attended, some not. Here is a random selection:

May 1972: John Angus

An excellent crowd of 16,059 turned out at Turf Moor for the Clarets' long-serving full-back. Angus was the last member of the title winning side of 1959/60, and the gate was more than 2,000 over the average gate. On a celebratory evening, the Second Division trophy went to skipper Martin Dobson.

6 May 2007: Graham Branch

Just 1,809 souls turned out for Graham Branch at the end of the 2006/07 season. Ex-teammates Adrian Heath, David Eyres, Ian Cox and Ian Moore played and it proved to be an entertaining afternoon for a Clarets stalwart who had served the club for eight-and-a-half years. Branch was on target, too, as he scored the sort of goal every player dreams of – faux challenges and players swooned as he burst through to score in the sixty-fifth minute. Burnley drew 3-3 with Branch's All Star XI.

30 August 2004: Stan Ternent

Former boss Stan Ternent walked out to a nearly half-full Turf Moor for his tribute game in August 2004. Playing a strong Manchester United XI, the Clarets lost 3-1 in front of 9,000 supporters who gave their former manager a standing ovation. The game saw the likes of

Tim Howard, Phil Neville, Eric Djemba-Djemba, Bellion, Ryan Giggs and Paul Scholes in action for the Reds. Goals from Scholes, Neville and Eagles opened up a sizeable advantage for the visitors, though Marc Pugh pulled a consolation back for the Clarets.

8 August 1991: Jimmy Holland

Burnley took on Oldham Athletic for Clarets physiotherapist Jimmy Holland, an excellent servant to the club and a fantastic character. With a decent turnout of 4,151, Graham Lancashire put the hosts ahead after just two minutes as two full-strength teams treated the game as anything but a stroll in the park. Latics hit back when substitute Paul Kane scored in the seventy-first and eighty-seventh minutes to secure a hard-fought win that proved a fitting tribute to the watching Holland.

Other games...

The Clarets provided Liverpool with the opposition for three testimonials in the space of three years in the late nineteenth century. All the games were played at Anfield for McGregor, Joe McQue and Malcolm McVean, which ended thus:

8 January 1894	*v*. Liverpool	lost 2-0	McGregor	Att: 300
6 April 1896	*v*. Liverpool	lost 4-3	Joe McQue	Att: 5000
12 April 1897	*v*. Liverpool	drew 1-1	Malcolm McVean	Att: N/A

SUPER CALLY ARE ATROCIOUS, BURNLEY ARE FANTASTIC

Inverness Caledonian Thistle were the visitors to Turf Moor on 2 August 2008 as the Clarets wrapped up the pre-season preparations. A crowd of 4,406 saw the hosts score twice in the three minutes just before the break, thanks to Wade Elliot and Chris Eagles. Though

Barrowman pulled a goal back on sixty-five minutes, Burnley saw the game out to win 2-1.

The teams that day were:

Burnley: Penny (Jensen 69), Alexander, Duff, Caldwell (Carlisle 69), Kalvenes (Jordan 54), van der Schaaf (McDonald 69), McCann (Gudjonsson 46), Elliott (Jones 73), Eagles (Mahon 78), Blake (Solovjovs 73), Paterson (Akinbiyi 69). Subs: Berisha, Kay.

Inverness CT: Fraser, Tokely, McGuire (Duff 64), Munro, Hastings, Cowie, Black, Duncan, McBain (Imrie 64), Barrowman, Rooney (McAllister 79). Subs: Djebi-Zadi, Proctor, Wilson, Vigurs, Wood, Esson.

CULT HERO NO. 3: TOMMY LAWTON

The legendary Tommy Lawton is still a great source of pride for Clarets fans. One of the game's most prolific scorers and all-time greats began his career at Turf Moor, and though his stay was relatively brief, Burnley fans watched the teenage protégé's career like a proud parent, as he broke various records on the way to becoming a national idol.

Born in Farnworth, Lancashire, Lawton's precocious talent won him a trial for the England schoolboy team in which he scored a hat-trick, though he would never win a full junior cap despite his obvious talent. In 1935, aged sixteen, he joined Burnley, then in the Second Division, and worked in a tannery in Bolton, despite signing amateur forms.

Talking of his early days with the Clarets, Lawton later wrote,

I remember my first meeting with Hughie Gallacher. It was after I had had a bad game for Burnley Reserves against Derby County Reserves. I was walking off the pitch with my heart in my boots when Hughie, who was the Derby centre forward, came up to me and said, 'Look, son, you must learn to cover the ball with your body. If you are being tackled on your right, keep the ball on your left foot, so your opponent will have to come across you to get at it, and it's the same the other way round. If you do that they won't take it from you.' I shall never forget the great Hughie Gallacher for that.

With the advice firmly on board, Lawton, who had flat feet and needed to wear orthotics, progressed at a rate of knots and after a year with Burnley, Lawton turned professional and became the youngest player in club history to represent the first team, when he made his debut aged sixteen years and 163 days old against Doncaster Rovers. He underlined his promise with a hat-trick at home to Tottenham Hotspur four days after his seventeenth birthday in October 1936.

Such raw talent was always going to attract attention, and with Everton searching for a replacement for the ageing Dixie Dean, the Toffees came calling for the Clarets' precocious talent. With sixteen goals in twenty-five games, Lawton was gone for a fee of £6,500.

He would go on to score goals by the bucketful for every club he played for – Everton, Chelsea, Notts County, Brentford and Arsenal, as well as twenty-two in twenty-three games for England. The Second World War stole seven years of his peak years, and one can only guess how many goals the former Claret would have scored had he not missed so many games. As it is, he'll just have to make do with being a legend of the game and a cult hero at Turf Moor.

SHOTS IN THE DARK

Though the Clarets took the 1991/92 Division Four title, things could have gone badly pear-shaped as events threatened to transpire against the club. The Clarets were one of the first clubs to play Aldershot twice during the campaign, having met in August and then again just before Christmas. But when the Shots were forced to resign from the Football League midway through the campaign, the 2-0 home win and the 2-1 away win were both wiped from the record books, along with six precious points. The goalscorers also saw their goals erased from history, but we record them here for posterity.

24 August 1991	Aldershot (H)	2–0	Conroy, Francis	5,877
21 December 1991	Aldershot (A)	2–1	Harper, Lancashire	2,574

THE ORIGINAL INVINCIBLES

The Clarets would never dream of doing things the easy way, so in preparation to enter the history books in 1920/21, the club lost the first three games of the campaign – all against South Yorkshire opposition in the form of Bradford City (twice), and Huddersfield Town to sit firmly on the foot of the table. Burnley then went on a run of thirty league games without defeat – a record that would stand for more than eighty years before Arsenal's 'Invincibles' topped that run in 2003/04. Yet, it seemed as though the Clarets may have run out of steam towards the end of the campaign. The run came to an end at Hyde Road where title rivals Manchester City triumphed 3-0. Though the Clarets then beat Manchester United, then City in the next two games, John Haworth's side failed to win any of their remaining six games, drawing three and losing three – but one of those draws at Everton saw Burnley crowned top-flight champions for the first time in the club's history.

THEY SAID IT...

First, some entertaining quotes from the man who took Burnley back to the Premier League, Sean Dyche. Life's a shoe-in for big Sean Dyche:

> I don't have an Imelda Marcos obsession, but I love a good pair of hand-made leather shoes. I have an affinity with shoes because I grew up where I did and as a kid I always had hand-made leather shoes even for

school, so it's an appreciation. Then a pair of shoes would last 20 years. Now it's buy cheap, buy twice. It's sad how the shoe-making industry has declined.

Big Sean on making his own luck:

I have worked very hard to make my life what it is. I love Gary Player's quote 'the harder I work the luckier I become. Fortune favours the prepared.' I like that.

Glad Sean said this!

What would you change about myself? My ginger hair. No, my volume. I'm very loud, but I can't be anything else. If I try to talk quietly, it doesn't sound authentic, in fact I sound like a weirdo.

Martin Dobson pays tribute to Jimmy Holland in June 2006:

Nobody likes to be injured but when you are you need someone to lift your spirits and also you need someone who is professional enough so you have complete confidence in whatever they say about your treatment. In Jimmy you had both of those things. He was a great person and he was a great character. He was so well respected by the boys.

Charlie Austin, May 2013 – who left with his held high two months later:

I think every boy growing up wants to be a professional footballer. When that chance comes, every footballer wants to play in the Premier League. Every footballer wants that chance. If I get the chance, so be it. If it comes this summer I'll take it, and I'll leave Burnley Football Club with my head held high.

Sean gears up for promotion in 2014:

League tables are for fans to look at and the media to speculate about. I am much more interested in performances, and getting the preparation right for the next game. I won promotion four times as a player, and I'm not going to deny I would enjoy another one as a manager, but you can ask any of the clubs I went up with and they will tell you the same. My focus was always dead calm, always on the next game.

Diplomatic, grounded and intelligent – Sean Dyche, 2014:

Football is a business like any other and stuff like that happens. My brother works at Weetabix in Kettering. That was taken over, there were redundancies. My other brother is a builder who has lost jobs, lost work. Football is not immune from that, it just happens to be in more of a spotlight. I had eight or nine really good years at Watford, as a player, a captain, youth coach, reserve coach, first team coach, assistant manager and then manager. Why would I choose not to remember all that over one thing that didn't go in my favour?

BHOYS WILL BE BOYS

The Anglo-Scottish Cup looked anything but a pre-season friendly tournament when Burnley took on Celtic at Turf Moor, with a violent encounter off the pitch.

The Glaswegians came to Lancashire in their thousands – 10,000 to be exact – though the Clarets' idea to let players kick blue and white balls into the stands before the game was probably not the best idea, being the colours of arch-rivals Rangers.

The Tartan masses arrived early, and many had been drinking for much of the day, so there was always the chance that things could turn nasty. The Clarets fans taunted the Celtic contingent with shouts of 'Rangers' ending in the visiting fans breaking into an area of segregation separating the two sets of fans and only the intervention of police with dogs stopped the two sets of supporters clashing.

The Celtic fans tore up iron railings and used them as missiles as the club's good name was besmirched with Superintendent Henderson of Lancashire police claiming it was the worst hooliganism he had experienced, with sixty people injured, including several police.

Referee Pat Partridge had to withdraw the players for a period until order was restored, while Celtic boss Billy McNeill and his players appealed to the fans for calm. Justice was done when Steve Kindon scored what would be the only goal of the game on fifty-five minutes to seal a 1-0 win in front of 25,000 fans.

The teams that day were:

Burnley: Stevenson, Scott, Brennan, Noble, Thomson, Rodaway, Cochrane, Hall, Fletcher, Kindon, James. Subs: Smith, Norman.
Celtic: Latchford, Fillipi, Lynch, Aitken, Edvaldsson, Glavin, Doyle, Conroy, McAdam, Burns, McCluskey. Subs: McGrain, Baines.
Referee: Mr P. Partridge (Bishop Auckland)
Attendance: 25,000

THE MANAGERS
NO. 5: JOHN HAWORTH 1910–24

Though R. H. Wadge took the managerial reins on an interim basis following the tragic death of Spen Whittaker, Accrington secretary John Haworth was appointed as permanent boss in July 1910. Haworth's arrival hardly captured the imagination of Clarets fans, who believed he had little experience or track record to speak of. For many, a continuation of the second tier mediocrity beckoned for Burnley, who had failed to make a real impression in English football.

But Haworth would have an immense effect on the club's fortune. Despite a decent eight-place finish in his first campaign, Haworth decided to make a change that would change the DNA of Burnley FC forever – he ditched the club colours of green, which he considered (with plenty of evidence to back up his theory) to be unlucky. So in the summer of 1911, Haworth convinced the board to switch to the colours of Aston Villa, the club who were dominating English football at the time, and played in the more attractive colours of claret and blue. He also added centre-half Tommy Boyle from Barnsley to lead his new-look side, and the club was effectively reborn.

The transformation was immediate as the Clarets finished third in 1911/12, and then won promotion back to the top flight in 1912/13 by finishing runners-up in Division Two, while also reaching the FA Cup semi-finals. A season of consolidation followed with a twelfth place finish in the First Division, but it would prove a historic campaign as Burnley FC won a first major honour, beating Liverpool 1-0 in the 1914 FA Cup final at the Crystal Palace. Haworth had finally put the Clarets very firmly on the map.

The following season in 1914/15 saw the club finish fourth in the table, and it seemed there would be a period of glory for Haworth's side, but the First World War interrupted, and football was forced to take a four-year break. But the Clarets somehow kept their momentum after the resumption of league football, finishing runners-up in 1919/20 and then – at last – champions in 1920/21. The town celebrated in style, and with crowds averaging more than 30,000, it was a golden era for the club. Though a third place finish ensured the Clarets remained one of the nation's top sides, a slow decline in fortunes had begun, with finishes of fifteenth and seventeenth over the next two seasons. The club were in eighteenth position going into December 1924 when tragedy once again. Haworth, aged only forty-eight, caught pneumonia and died on 4 December, meaning – incredibly – the club had lost two successive managers in tragic circumstances. Haworth's death sent the town into mourning once again, but his legacy gave Burnley a new identity, a First Division title and FA Cup – he remains one of the Clarets' greatest managers.

CLARETS GET THE BLUES

Burnley manager John Bond effectively turned the Clarets into a Manchester City retirement home after being appointed boss in 1983. Bond had managed City from 1980 to 1983, before quitting Maine Road after a 4-0 FA Cup defeat at Brighton. He elected to bring experienced players with him, adding no less than seven City veterans for the 1983/84 campaign, including Gerry Gow, Tommy Hutchison, Willie Donachie, Kevin Reeves, Dennis Tueart, Wayne Biggins and Kevin Glendon.

LOVE THY NEIGHBOURS

When Accrington Stanley were facing bankruptcy, Owen Coyle's Clarets stepped in to help their stricken neighbours. The two clubs, just a few miles apart, but never having met competitively, played on 8 September 2009. A crowd of 5,301 turned out on a wet night at Turf Moor, but the gesture was greatly appreciated by the travelling support of around 1,000 who chanted 'we love you Burnley' at one point. For the record, the Clarets won 4-0 with goals from Fernando Guerrero, a Chris Eagles free-kick and a Jay Rodriguez brace.

The starting line-ups were:

Burnley: Penny; Easton, Edgar, Duff, Eckersley; Guerrero, McDonald, Eagles; Rodriguez, Thompson, Nugent. Subs: McDonald, Anderson, Harvey, Wes Fletcher, Hoskin.

Accrington Stanley: Martin; Lloyd, Kempson, Ami, Murphy; Miles, Proctor, Melow, Turner; King, McConville. Subs: Dunbavin, Symes, Black/Riley, Joyce/Grant, Richardson.

BADGE OF HONOUR

OK, have you ever wondered what the Clarets' badge is all about? Well here's what it all breaks down to, according to the excellent 'Clarets Mad' website. The knight's helmet apparently represents two knighted families of the area, the Townleys and the Shuttleworths of Gawthorpe (but you already know that, right?). The cotton thread (see what I did there?) is down to the cotton heritage of the town, the Lancashire rose is pretty self-explanatory. Of course, lions didn't once roam East Lancashire – the lion on the badge represents England and the fact Turf Moor was the first League ground to be visited by a member of the Royal family. The hand represents the hand of friendship and the town motto 'Held to the Truth', while the bee, often associated to Manchester, is believed to be because the club was seen as being 'busy as a bee' as well as the Bee Hole End Stand. Not sure about the bee bit...

FA CUP

The FA's ruling that professionalism was a no-no did not deter Burnley FC who were made of sterner stuff and would eventually pave the way for footballers being able to earn a living from the game. The Clarets paid some of their squad so the FA insisted that the club's first FA Cup tie could only go ahead if a reserve side full of amateurs played against Darwen – the result would prove to be a record defeat, with Darwen winning 11-0. We would have our revenge against said opposition, though...

SEVENTIES HITS

In the Clarets' fanzine *Forever and a Day*, the ten most popular chants of the 1970s were listed thus:

- 'We Are the Burnley Boot Boys'
- 'Hark Now Hear the Burnley Sing'
- 'Stevie, Stevie Kindon, Steve Kindon On the Wing'
- 'Ee Aye, Ee Aye, Ee Aye Oh, Up the Football League We Go'
- 'We Hate Nottingham Forest, We Hate Liverpool Too…'
- 'No Nay Never'
- 'I Was Born Under a Claret Star'
- 'Oh Ralphie Coates (Is Wonderful)'
- 'Tiptoe Through the Longside'
- 'In Our Lancashire Homes'

THE HISTORY BOYS

The Clarets began life by losing their first league game to Preston North End. A 5-2 loss at Deepdale was hardly the beginning the players, officials and fans had hoped for, but those taking part etched their name into club history forever.

The starting XI were Smith, Lang, Bury, Abrams, Friel, Keenan, Brady, Tait, Poland, Gallocher, Yates. The goals came from Gallocher and Poland.

Things were looking up a week later when Burnley gave a glimpse of a possible future in a rollercoaster game at home to Bolton Wanderers – the hosts went in 0-3 down at the break but staged a remarkable recovery to win 4-3 and register their first two points. The goals came from Poland and Tait.

CLARETS SONG AND CHANT SELECTIONS

'Oh, Me Lads'
Oh the lads, you should have seen 'em coming,
Running down the Brunshaw Road the Burnley boys are coming,
All the lads and lasses with their smiles upon their faces,
Running down the Brunshaw Road, to see the Burnley aces!

'Look Away'
Oh I wish I was in the town of cotton,
Good times there are not forgotten,
Look away, look away, look away Clarets fans,
I wish I was at Turf Moor, Burnley, Burnley,
I wish I was at Turf you know,
To stand once more with the Longside Row,
Away, away, away and home with Burnley!

'Just Can't Get Enough'
When I see you Burnley, I go out of my head,
I just can't get enough, I just can't get enough,
All the things you do to me, and all the things you say,
I just can't get enough, I just can't get enough,
We slip and slide as we fall in love and I just can't seem
to get enough.

'Come to Ewood, Come to Ewood'
It's a place of misery,
There's a notice on the doorstep saying 'welcome unto thee',
Don't believe 'em,
Don't believe 'em, 'cause it's all a pack of lies,
If it weren't for ******d Rovers, we would be in paradise.

'Can't help falling in Love'
Take my hand; take my whole life through, for I can't help falling in love with you.
Take my hand, take my whole life through, for I can't help falling in love with you.
The Burnley (Clap clap clap)
The Burnley (Clap clap clap)

'In Our Lancashire Homes'
In our Lancashire homes, we speak with an accent exceedingly rare.
The Longside of Burnley will always be there,
In our Lancashire homes.

'We're Up all Night'
We're up all night for Sam Vokes
We're up all night for Dave Jones
We're up all night for Heat-on
We're up all night for Dean Marney
We're up all night for Dean Marney
We're up all night for Dean Marney
Dean Marney, Dean Marney Marney Marney
Dean Marney, Dean Marney Marney Marney
Dean Marney, Dean Marney Marney Marney
All night long, Dean Marney
All night long, Dean Marney
All night long, Dean Marney

'Fight For Your Right'
You've gotta fight!
For your right!
DEAN MAAAAAAAAAAAAAAAAARNEY!

'We Are the Longside'
Bertie Mee said to Bill Shankly, 'have you heard of the north bank Highbury?'
Shanks said 'No I don't think so, but I've heard the Longside, Burnley.'
Were the Longside Burnley, were the Longside Burnley...

JACK IN THE BOX

John 'Jack' Yates was able to put a disappointing Clarets season behind him when he was called up by England for the match against Ireland in March 1889. Yates couldn't have wished for a better start for his country as he scored a hat-trick in a 6-1 win over the Irish during the match at Anfield. It should have been the start of a glittering career for Yates, but six weeks later, he wasn't selected for the game against Scotland and never represented England again. He remains the only England player to average three goals, and is one of only five England players to score a hat-trick on his debut. He played occasionally for the Clarets thereafter, but eventually returned to his trade in the cotton industry where he worked as a weaver.

UP FOR THE CUP

Burnley lifted a first-ever trophy in the 1889/90 season, when they won the Lancashire Senior Cup, beating Blackburn Rovers 2-0 courtesy of two Alex Stewart goals. The Clarets wouldn't win the competition again until 1914/15, but had to then wait thirty-five years for further success in the 1949/50 campaign, and a fourth triumph quickly followed in 1951/52. From 1959 to 1962, the Clarets successfully defended the Lancashire Cup for three seasons, winning it again in 1964/65 and 1965/66 to make it five wins from a possible six – the 1962/63 competition was not completed. There have been three more titles since in 1969/70, 1971/72 and 1992/93 – the thirteenth and last time the old trophy resided at Turf Moor. For the record, our neighbours Blackburn Rovers have won it once more than the Clarets and Bolton one less.

TOP TRANSFER FEES PAID

It's a sobering thought that the Clarets' top nine transfer fees paid amount to less than Cristiano Ronaldo's annual pay. Up to June 1 2014, Steven Fletcher's £3 million price tag remained the top fee paid by the club, and that was back in 2005. With promotion to the Premier League in 2013/14 achieved, and a windfall estimated to be somewhere close to £100 million, expect this list to change dramatically in the very near future.

Player	From	Fee	Date
1 Steven Fletcher	Hibernian	£3 million	July 2009
2 André Bikey	Reading	£2.8 million	July 2009
3 Danny Fox	Celtic	£1.8 million	January 2010
4 Leon Cort	Stoke City	£1.5 million	January 2010
5 Chris Eagles	Manchester U	£1.2 million	July 2008
6 Ian Moore	Stockport C	£1 million	November 2000
6 Robbie Blake	Bradford City	£1 million	January 2002
6 Martin Paterson	Scunthorpe U	£1 million	June 2008
9 Steve Davis	Luton Town	£850,000	December 1998

MORE FOOL US?

Playing on 1 April has been no joke for Burnley over the years. With just one win in thirty-six years, it's not a date Clarets fans have enjoyed historically. The last three games on this date have ended in draws with Nottingham Forest, Sheffield Wednesday and Portsmouth, but without doubt the most painful defeat was a 5-0 defeat at Ewood Park in 2001. The last victory was a 2-1 win over Cardiff City in 2000, and the complete record is: Played 26, Won 7, Drawn 9, Lost 10, Scored 32, Conceded 40.

INCREDIBLE START

Matt Busby's Manchester United were the FA Cup third round opponents in January 1954, and the clamour to be inside Turf Moor to see the Busby Babes in action was at a premium. The queues around the ground were so long that hundreds were still outside by the time the game kicked off – those still outside were about to miss one of the most incredible starts ever seen at the Turf. Les Shannon scored for Burnley in the first sixty seconds, and Bill Holden doubled the hosts' lead not long after to leave the majority of the 52,000 crowd in raptures – and those outside cursing their luck! United hit back in stunning style by scoring twice in the next two minutes through Dennis Violet and a Jock Aird own goal to make it 2-2 with seven minutes on clock. Breathless stuff! The Clarets restored their lead through Shannon before the break, but United hit back in the second half when Ernie Taylor levelled. But the Clarets finished strongly with Jimmy McIlroy and Billy Gray scoring to give the hosts a famous 5-3 win.

ISLE OF MAN

The Clarets were the victims of arguably the Manx national team's most famous win when the Isle of Man beat Burnley 1-0 in July 2000 as part of the Steam Packets Tournament. Remember, no man is an island, unless it's the Isle of Man.

CITY GENT

Gerry Creaney was having a torrid time at Manchester City, so when the former Portsmouth and Celtic man was offered the chance of a loan spell with Burnley, he jumped the opportunity – and proved what a top striker he could be. Though he failed to find the net in his first three games, he scored two in each of his next two games and added four in the final six games of his two-month loan spell. The Clarets couldn't afford the wages Creaney was being paid and the striker returned to Maine Road, but with a legion of new admirers after his eight goals in ten games.

JIMMY GRUMBLE

Jimmy Robson wrote his name into the record books when he scored five goals during the Clarets' 8-0 win over Nottingham Forest at Turf Moor in November 1959. Despite this sizeable feat, Robson was far from an idol amongst the Burnley supporters, and his goal haul did little to change the minds of the majority of fans. Poor Jimmy battled on from 1956–65, and made more than 200 appearances before leaving for pastures new.

HOW CAN YOU FINISH THIRD IN THE FA CUP?

Perhaps a decent quiz question if you're with your mates down the pub – who finished third in the 1974 FA Cup competition? As interesting as the World Cup third and fourth place play-off, in 1969 the FA, in their infinite wisdom, decided to introduce this game as a prelude to the final itself. With the Clarets suffering a semi-final heartbreak against Newcastle United, the prospect of playing Leicester in this most meaningless of matches hardly whetted the appetite. Worse still, the match was played five days after the final, meaning interest was at a maximum low. Scheduled to play at Turf Moor, the re-laying of a new pitch meant the match had to be switched to Filbert Street and the Foxes fans – marginally less interested than their Burnley counterparts – voted with their feet with a paltry 6,548 bothering to turn out. Those who did left disappointed as Ray Hankin's goal settled the match and the Clarets became the last side to finish third in the FA Cup.

The full list of third- and fourth-place play-off games:

1969/70 FA Cup, 10 April 1970
Manchester United 2-0 Watford
Highbury
15,105

1970/71 FA Cup, 7 May 1971
Stoke City 3-2 Everton
Selhurst Park
5,031

1971/72 FA Cup, 5 August 1972
Birmingham City 0-0 Stoke City
(4–3 pens to Birmingham)
St Andrew's
25,841

1972/73 FA Cup, 18 August 1973
Wolves 3-1 Arsenal
Highbury
21,038

1973/74 FA Cup, 9 May 1974
Burnley 1-0 Leicester City
Filbert Street
6,458

THE SHORTEST SEASON

The 1939/40 season was Burnley's shortest ever, and was over after just two games. The Clarets began the campaign with a decent 1-1 draw with Coventry City at Turf Moor of August 26 1939, and a week later travelled to St Andrew's to face Birmingham City, where Blues won 2-0 to leave Burnley second bottom. The day after, Prime Minister Neville Chamberlain announced to the nation that Britain was at war with Germany and all football, except for wartime and regional matches, was immediately suspended for the next seven years. While the Clarets technically went seven years and five months without a win – beating Birmingham City 2-0 at St Andrew's – imagine how Swansea Town must have felt, losing 8-1 to Newcastle United before war broke out. That's a long time to get something like that out of your system! Incidentally, the rematch ended 1-1 in 1946.

TEXACO CUP

The forerunner to the Anglo-Scottish Cup was the Texaco Cup, which involved teams from England, Northern Ireland, the Republic of Ireland and Scotland who had not qualified for European competition in their respective nations.

Irish and Northern Irish clubs withdrew from the competition after 1971/72 due to political pressure and ongoing troubles in Northern Ireland. They eventually entered a short-lived all-Irish version of the competition. As you may have gathered from the name, the tournament was sponsored by American petroleum giant Texaco, who pumped in around £100,000 in prize money, chiefly to gain brand recognition in the UK and also to help promote their recent purchase of the Regent filling station chain. In 1975, the name changed to the Anglo-Scottish Cup after the withdrawal of Texaco's sponsorship.

The Clarets went goal crazy in the opening two rounds of the Cup, beating East Fife 7-0 at Turf Moor, and then 3-2 in the somewhat meaningless second leg. The goal glut continued with the dismantling of Edinburgh-based Hearts 3-0 win at Tynecastle, and a 5-0 second leg romp at Turf Moor – eighteen goals in just four games. Norwich proved stiffer opposition in the semi-finals, but the Clarets still marched on, winning the home leg 2-0 and then beating the Canaries 3-2 at Carrow Road for good measure. Though a two-legged final was planned at the start of the competition, it was reduced to a one-off game at St James' Park, where Newcastle triumphed 2-1 in extra time in front of more than 25,000 fans.

This cross-border tournament's official name was the International League Board Competition, but thanks to the sponsor, was retitled the Texaco Cup. Entrants were restricted to those clubs that had just missed out on gaining a place in one of the three European club competitions. Sixteen clubs (six each from Scotland and England, and four from Ireland) entered the first series, but by 1972 the Irish sides were dropped due to the political unrest at the time. The last season saw the English part of the draw increase to sixteen clubs drawn into four qualifying sections.

Each entrant was to receive cash sums depending on the round reached:

First round £1,000–£1,500
Second round £2,000
Finalists £2,500
Winners £3,500

1970/71

First Round

Morton-West Bromwich Albion	2-1	1-0	3-1	
Motherwell-Stoke City	1-0	1-2	2-2	aet 4-3p
Nottingham Forest-Airdrieonians	2-2	2-2	4-4	aet 4-5p
Burnley-Heart of Midlothian	3-1	1-4	4-5	
Dundee-Wolverhampton Wanderers	1-2	0-0	1-2	

Tottenham Hotspur-Dunfermline Athletic	4-0	3-0	7-0
Ards-Shamrock Rovers	1-4	3-2	4-6
Limerick-Derry City	1-0	2-4	3-4

1973/74

First Round

Burnley-East Fife	7-0	3-2	10-2	
Everton-Heart of Midlothian	0-1	0-0	0-1	
Sheffield United-Dundee United	0-0	0-2	0-2	
Ayr United-Leicester City	1-1	0-2	1-3	
Morton-Newcastle United	1-2	1-1	2-3	aet
St Johnstone-Norwich City	0-2	0-1	0-3	
Stoke City-Birmingham City	0-0	0-0	0-0	aet 4-5p
Coventry City-Motherwell	0-1	2-3	2-4	

Second Round

Birmingham City-Newcastle United	1-1	1-3	2-4
Norwich City-Motherwell	2-0	1-0	3-0
Heart of Midlothian-Burnley	0-3	0-5	0-8
Leicester City-Dundee United	1-1	0-1	1-2

Semi-finals

Burnley-Norwich City	2-0	3-2	5-2	
Dundee United-Newcastle United	2-0	1-4	3-4	aet

Final

24 April 1974: Newcastle 2-1 Burnley, Att 34,540

THEY SAID IT...

Interesting and memorable quotes about, or by, Stan Ternent. Neil Warnock, in typically blunt fashion, slates our beloved Stan:

The two managers I really dislike are Stan Ternent and Gary Megson. The old saying that I wouldn't p**s on them if they were on fire applies.

Stan Ternent tells reporters what he will bring to the Clarets shortly after being appointed by Burnley:

What you will get from Burnley is an organisation, an endeavour, a commitment and a will to win as well as no fear of losing.

Brian 'The Beast' Jensen praises his former boss, 2013:

You could easily learn something from him – but he was definitely old school. If something didn't suit him he would let you know and do his very best to get his wish, his command, otherwise you're out the door. I was always fascinated by him and on top of that he was the nicest man in the world.

Stan Ternent, 2001:

It can be both a burden and an inspiration. I'm 55 now and I've known Burnley from the good days. I know what Burnley is about, as a club and as a town. It is amazing how many former players come back and live in the town. I understand that. I understand the history - sometimes it might be easier if I didn't.

THE MANAGERS
NO. 6: ALBERT PICKLES, 1924–32

Albert Pickles knew he had a thankless task following in the footsteps of Burnley's greatest manager, John Haworth. A director at Turf Moor since 1918, Pickles had trials with Aston Villa as a youngster and was a decent player, but fate had taken him down a different path and he now found himself in charge of the Clarets.

He managed to keep the club afloat, despite struggling against relegation from the moment he took over, and a quartet of new signings gave new hope for supporters keen to see their side challenge at the top once again. Those hopes were given a massive reality check when the Clarets lost the opening game of the 1925/26 season 10-0 at Aston Villa. Pickles was in a pickle, but he showed his powers of rejuvenation as he rallied his team to bounce back with a 4-0 win over Leicester in the next game. The tone set, Burnley struggled all season and only wins over Spurs and Cardiff in the final two games saw relegation avoided by one point.

Burnley clawed back some pride the following season with a fifth place finish, but successive nineteenth place finishes saw the Clarets again escape relegation by the skin of their teeth. The inevitable happened in 1929/30 with relegation back to the second tier for the first time in seventeen years. There was to be no immediate return either, and after finishing eighth in 1930/31, there was a narrow escape from relegation to the Third Division North, avoided by just two points in 1931/32. With Pickles' stock at an all-time low, only a confident start to the 1932/33 campaign could save his job, and when Preston North End thrashed the Clarets 6-1 on the second match of the season, Pickles offered his resignation, which was accepted by the board.

BUZZER REWARD

Having left for Burnley just a few months earlier in 1975, Mike Summerbee was granted a testimonial with Manchester City after almost ten years of sterling service with the Blues. A crowd of 20,309 paid tribute to Buzzer, who played in an entertaining 4-3 defeat to Manchester United.

CHRISTMAS CRACKERS

The Clarets played their last Christmas Day fixture in 1957, when they beat Manchester City 2-1 at Turf Moor. After that, Christmas Day games became a thing of the past, but Burnley were one of the few clubs who were probably sad to see the festive fixtures end, due to the excellent record the club had on that day.

The first game was a 4-1 win over Sheffield United, and the Clarets remained unbeaten until 1913, when Sunderland ended a run of eight wins and two draws – Blackpool were the opposition in seven of those games. Curiously, Turf Moor hosted no less than thirty-five of the thirty-eight Christmas Day games played, and none of the away fixtures were won. The complete record for games played on 25 December is: Played 38, Won 22, Drawn 9, Lost 7, Scored 77, Conceded 44.

THE MANAGERS
NO. 7: TOM BROMILOW, 1932–35

The Clarets were happy to be managerless for several weeks following the departure of Albert Pickles. Indeed, the team recorded successive 4-0 wins and two draws following Pickles' departure, but then the form fell away and Tom Bromilow was offered the position.

The first Burnley manager to have actually played professionally, Bromilow had been coaching in Holland and he was also the first boss to be recruited from outside the immediate locale. Twice a title winner with Liverpool, he had played more than 300 league games and won five England caps, so his pedigree and standing within the game was without question – but did he have the wherewithal to resurrect a sleeping giant in his first management role? The answer was not really. There was no improvement on the previous season's nineteenth place finish, and he set about rebuilding the team for the following game, including the purchase of veteran former Aston Villa and Huddersfield striker George Brown – a prolific striker who arrived with a record of 221 goals in 339 games. Brown didn't disappoint at Turf Moor, scoring twenty-seven goals in forty-one appearances during the 1934/35 season, though even his goals didn't inspire a promotion challenge during Bromilow's somewhat disappointing reign, and the manager left his post in 1935.

RECORD SIGNINGS

Here is a list of the Clarets' big-money signings from the recent past:

	Player	From	Fee	Date
1	Steven Fletcher	Hibernian	£3 million	July 2009
2	André Bikey	Reading	£2.8 million	July 2009
3	Danny Fox	Celtic	£1.8 million	January 2010
4	Leon Cort	Stoke City	£1.5 million	January 2010
5	Chris Eagles	Manchester	£1.2 million	July 2008
6	Ian Moore	Stockport County	£1 million	November 2000
=	Robbie Blake	Bradford City	£1 million	January 2002
=	Martin Paterson	Scunthorpe U	£1 million	June 2008
9	Steve Davis	Luton Town	£850,000	December 1998

THE MANAGERS
NO. 8: ALF BOLAND, 1935–40

The failed experiment with Bromilow saw a return to looking for a manager closer to home. Alf Boland was a figurehead, with the

Burnley board selecting the team via committee – normally, never a good approach! Boland was the link between board and team, but he was young, had little experience at management level and his tenure was far from spectacular, though he did give a debut to promising youngster Tommy Lawton and also purchased Arthur Woodruff, along with talented youngsters George Bray and Harry Potts. Boland was in the process of assembling a more than useful side when war broke out and, as many other managers and players did around that time, he drifted away from the game and left the club a year later as matters greater than football took over everyday life.

THE MANAGERS
NO. 9: CLIFF BRITTON, 1945–48

Once described by the legendary Everton striker, Dixie Dean, as the best crosser of a ball in the game, Cliff Britton's esteemed playing career came to end during the war. Often described as a skilful and classy playmaker, Britton's career blossomed at Goodison Park and he became a firm favourite with the Toffees' fans – but could he turn those silky skills to management?

Though he took over before the cessation of the Second World War, with the Clarets still playing in the Football League North, Britton proved he was ahead of his time by presenting a blueprint to the board of how he intended to take the Clarets back to the top division. Despite his attacking instincts, Britton believed if he could construct a defence that was difficult to breach, the club's fortunes would greatly improve. With that in mind, he fashioned a back line of steel, who went out each week with the intention of preventing the opposition scoring. It worked like a charm, with just twenty-nine goals conceded in forty-two games, helping clinch promotion at the first attempt as well as reaching the FA Cup final.

A new style, a team built around a defensive bedrock and Britton's insistence that he would bring through youngsters from the club's own system, Britton was like no other manager of the time and the Clarets were lucky to have him. Further evidence of the progress being made came during his second full season, when Burnley finished joint second in Division One, with only goal average putting Manchester United in second. Could he take the club to a second top flight title?

The answer would be no, as Britton's first love Everton came calling for his services, an offer he found impossible to refuse. Despite his departure, he had changed the way the club thought and restored pride to the Burnley supporters once again.

PROPER CHARLIE

In November 2012, Charlie Austin became the quickest Burnley player to reach the twenty-goal mark in a season when he smashed Andy Lochhead's record set in November 1966. Lochhead took twenty-five games to reach the landmark for the Clarets, while the prolific Austin shaved eight games off that tally by reaching twenty in just seventeen games when he bagged a late winner away to Leeds United.

Austin's father made a 550-mile round trip to see his son achieve the notable milestone as the player revealed after the game: 'He travelled up to watch from Bournemouth so he can have that one. To score twenty goals in a season is big, so I'm just happy with my overall performance at the moment.'

Austin scored hat-tricks against Peterborough and Sheffield Wednesday, and also equalled another Burnley record by scoring in eight consecutive appearances, though the run ended in the next match as Ipswich Town beat Sean Dyche's side 2-1.

UNWANTED RECORD

The Clarets set an unwanted Premier League record in April 2010, when they fell 3-0 down to Manchester City after just seven minutes at Turf Moor. In fact, it only equalled the record set by Oldham Athletic in 1993. In what was an extraordinary start to the game, Emmanuel Adebayor rifled in an Adam Johnson corner after four minutes, before Carlos Tevez fed Craig Bellamy, who slotted a second goal a minute later. Tevez then tapped in to put City three ahead after just seven minutes, with the Blues adding two more before the break to go in 5-0 to the good at the break. With rain pouring down onto a waterlogged Turf Moor pitch, the only glimmer of hope was that the game would be abandoned after the break, but referee Mike Wiley allowed what became something of a farce to continue with only Steven Fletcher's late goal giving the home fans something to cheer in a 6-1 defeat.

COTTON-PICKIN' RIVALS

If you were looking for a Rough Guide description or Idiots Guide to Derbies, the Clarets v Rovers derby would be described as thus: the East Lancashire Derby – also known in the past as the 'Cotton Mills Derby' but more lately 'El Lanclasico'. The first-ever competitive league match took place at Turf Moor on 3 November 1888, and Blackburn Rovers won the game 7–1. Blackburn also won the return fixture at Ewood Park 4–2 in what proved to be an inauspicious game. Only 11 miles separate the towns, with Accrington Stanley F.C. standing in the middle.

NAUGHTY BOYS

The Suicide Squad is a football hooligan firm linked to the Clarets. The self-imposed title is derived from previous behaviour at away games, where the single-minded involvement in violence against overwhelming odds could be described as suicidal. The name became synonymous with the group during the early 1980s, and many of the original members, now in their forties, are well known to the police and have a string of convictions for violence. Thankfully, violence is rarely seen at Turf Moor, though there is the odd altercation from time to time with visiting supporters.

THE MANAGERS
NO. 10: FRANK HILL, 1948–54

With an impressive playing career behind him, Frank Hill took over the reins at Turf Moor after leaving his post at Crewe Alexandra. The former triple title winner with Arsenal moved into coaching at Preston before becoming player/manager at Gretsy Road for the Railwaymen.

He arrived at Burnley in September 1948, and steadied the ship following Cliff Britton's departure. When he arrived, the club was in twentieth place, and he guided the Clarets to a safe if unspectacular fifteenth place finish. Just five defeats in the final seventeen games promised better things to come. By Boxing Day the following season, a point against Blackpool put the Clarets up to fourth and in with a chance of the title, but a poor second half of the campaign saw a tenth place finish.

Final placings of fourteenth, sixth and seventh followed to make Hill's tenure solid never threatening to trouble the trophy cabinet, but Hill was an astute judge of talent and brought in some fine players during his six-year stay. Billy Elliott, Roy Stephenson and Chelsea's Billy Gray all came to Turf Moor, but Hill will forever be revered as the man who brought Jimmy McIlroy to Burnley in March 1950.

Hill was informed of a raw young talent at Glentoran who may be worth a punt, and after seeing the player in action for himself, an £8,000 fee was agreed to bring McIlroy to Lancashire and a club legend was born.

Perhaps feeling he'd done all he could for the club and needing a fresh challenge, Hill returned to Preston in 1954, later taking up a scouting role for Manchester City, but he was always afforded a warm welcome on his return trips to Turf Moor.

MEAN MACHINE BREACHED

The Clarets went into the 1947 FA Cup final with Charlton – beaten finalists the season before – having kept twenty-five clean sheets during the 1946/47 campaign and not conceded more than one goal all season. Unfortunately, D-Day hero Chris Duffy's 114th-minute winner for Charlton proved to be the only goal of the game. Even Clarets fans agreed that a man who had stormed the beaches in Normandy just a few years before was worthy of such a momentous winner.

LUCKY ESCAPE

Burnley fans were nearly caught up in a disaster of epic proportions as they took on Liverpool at Ewood Park in the 1946/47 FA Cup semi-final. With demand at a premium to see the Clarets take on the champions-elect, hundreds of frustrated fans climbed over walls and turnstiles to gain entry, leading to crushing on the terraces. Dozens were stretchered to safety, and thankfully there were no fatalities. The incident was a chilling echo of the quarter-final at Burnden Park the season before when

Bolton took on Stoke and the desperation to see Stanley Matthews in action led to thousands of fans forcing their way in to the ground causing mayhem – thirty-three people died and more than 400 were injured.

THE MANAGERS
NO. 11: ALAN BROWN, 1954–57

Former Clarets skipper Alan Brown was delighted to accept the post of manager in 1954 following Frank Hill's departure, having cut his teeth in coaching having spent four years at Sheffield Wednesday.

His management style was based around defensive steel, much as he had been in his playing career. So the tough, uncompromising defender shaped a team in his image. The Clarets soon earned a reputation as a side who gave little away and the club was firmly established as a top flight team. Though his first season may have seen only a tenth-place finish, Burnley conceded fewer goals than any other side, including champions Chelsea – though the Clarets were also the lowest scorers.

Successive finishes of seventh again saw the defence among the best in the division. Brown was also instrumental in setting up the club's new Gawthorpe training ground, as well as bringing a number of talented players to the club. In 1957, he decided to take up an offer from Sunderland, but Brown, the tough disciplinarian who did things his way, had already laid the foundations for a glorious period that was just around the corner for the Clarets.

BUZZ IN, BUZZ OFF

OK, it's a well-used quiz question – which former Claret once played alongside Pele, Franz Beckenbauer and Sylvester Stallone? If you're thinking Peter Noble, think again. Of course, it is the one and only Mike Summerbee, who featured in *Escape to Victory* alongside the illustrious aforementioned trio. Buzzer may have only been at Turf Moor for eighteen months, from June 1975 to December 1976, but one of the legends of the late 1960s certainly gave his all for Burnley after signing from Manchester City for £35,000. True, his best days were behind him after more than 400 appearances for the Blues, but there were still flashes of genius from the former England winger. Summerbee moved to Turf Moor on the same day Willie Morgan joined from Manchester United, but despite the wealth of experience both men brought, the Clarets were still relegated at the end of the 1975/76 campaign. Buzzer remained at the club in the Second Division, but his contract was cancelled by mutual consent after a series of injuries saw him seek medical help in Manchester – but the treatment was refused by the Clarets and, after fifty-one appearances, the ex-City man moved to Blackpool for a brief spell before spending the last three years of his career with Stockport County.

BAD LUCK BLAKE

Robbie Blake's poor poker skills led to an underwear craze and a turn in fortunes for the popular striker after teammate, Clark Carlisle, purchased a pair of Y-fronts as a joke. Carlisle had the words 'Bad Beat Bob' printed onto the red undies and handed them to Blake after he'd lost a poker hand he allegedly should have won – when that happens, it's called a 'bad beat'. Blake decided to wear the gift and if he scored, reveal them to the world, which of course happened! Robbie scored against Coventry, the Y-fronts were exposed and the story spread in the media like wildfire. The Clarets' club shop stocked fifty pairs at £8.99 and they sold out within days. A spokesman for retail suggested they hadn't bought enough and had 'been caught with their pants down' – should have seen that coming.

HOW TWEET IT IS...

As of 1 June 2014, @BurnleyOfficial, the official Twitter account of Burnley FC, had just shy of 31,000 followers. At 4 p.m. on 31 May 2014 the club's official Facebook account had exactly 88,888 likes. There, nobody can say we're anti-social!

THEY SAID IT...

HRH Prince Charles reveals he has claret and blue blood:

> A consortium of my charities, including the British Asian Trust, have been working in Burnley. Hence, some of you asked this evening whether I support a British football club and I said 'yes – Burnley'.

Graham Alexander admits being left out of the side is hard to take, November 2009:

> Seeing others cross the white line and leaving you behind is the worst thing about being a footballer.

Brian Laws after his depleted side hold QPR 1-1 at Loftus Road, October 2009:

> We had six players violently ill. That's why it was an amazing performance and you have to give the lads great credit.

Brian 'The Beast' Jensen, who also sold his old banger for a newer model:

> They have a sausage in Burnley named 'The Beast' now! It's a shambles. A butcher turned up at the stadium with the biggest hot dog I have ever seen

and I've now got a couple of bags of sausages back home. It was funny at first but I did so many interviews about it that when I was asked to do another down at the butcher's shop I said no. It is time to concentrate on football, not sausages.

Brian Laws responds after the Clarets lose 6-1 at Turf Moor to Manchester City, who scored three in the first seven minutes, April 2010:

The first six minutes was extraordinary and embarrassing. It's not acceptable. If you give them time and space like that, Manchester City are going to hurt you - and they took maximum advantage. I gave them a right roasting at half-time, and laid down an objective to the players not to lose the second half. At least they did that. But the first six minutes killed it all, and all we can do is apologise and respond before we play Hull.

Sean Dyche reveals some of his management secrets, April 2014:

The modern train of thought is that suddenly there's a 'right way' of playing. I don't know who said that, I'm intrigued by it if I'm honest. If the so-called right way of playing is 500–700 passes a game and rolling out from the 'keeper and having 50–70 passes up to the other end and scoring, then you better have some good players. I have a pragmatic philosophy, I look at the group I've got, then I decide what strengths and weaknesses they have and then I formulate what I think is an appropriate way that those players can work in order to be individually and collectively successful to win games.

TalkSport presenter Adrian Durham, April 2014:

I was at Turf Moor to see Burnley secure promotion, and when the home fans voiced their admiration for manager Sean Dyche, they sang loud and proud: 'Ginger Mourinho.' What an insult. Not the ginger bit – there is nothing wrong with a bit of ginger. I mean the Mourinho bit. Pound for pound Dyche has been much better than Jose.

Boss Brian Miller enthuses before the 1988 Sherpa Van Trophy final *v.* Wolves:

This competition has been a god-send to us. We've sold all our tickets and I can't tell you what it's like to see Burnley alive and buzzing again.

THE MANAGERS
NO. 12: BILLY DOUGALL BROWN, 1957/58

With Alan Brown's departure on the eve of the 1957/58 season still sending shockwaves around Turf Moor, the board turned to former player and coach Billy Dougall, whose own career was cut short by injury. Dougall had been first team coach for more than twenty years, but many wondered if his chance hadn't come too late at the age of sixty-one. Indeed, suffering from ill health, Dougall was briefly hospitalised and eventually he had to accept he was in no fit state to manage the club, though was appointed physiotherapist until 1965 after reluctantly tendering his resignation but remained at Turf Moor. Though perhaps he isn't the first name thought of when club greats are mentioned, Dougall was a true unsung hero who more than played his part in this club's history.

SITE FOR SORE EYES

In April 2004, Clarets fan Paul Dale handed over the registered web domain of 'burnleyfc'. Dale, owner of the URL since 2000 decided to pass it over to the club because he 'wasn't doing anything with it'. In the early days of the internet, many official names were gobbled up by individuals who had a little more foresight than the organisations who would eventually come up to speed with such technicalities – many did so as possible avenues of income, but when intellectual property court cases were won, many were forced to hand over the rights. Dale, thankfully, was more than happy to pass on the name to his idols, adding, 'It's best with Burnley Football Club now and it's nice to know it will be some use and to see it every week on the club website.' Of course, today the official club site uses 'burnleyfootballclub.com' as the URL.

AH, I GET IT...

Former Clarets skipper Graham Branch once had a matchday programme column called 'Captain's Log' – branch ... log ... do you see what they did there? As with most skipper columns, it was a bit wooden...

CELEBRITY CLARETS

Financial expert and stand sponsor Dave Fishwick is a well-known Clarets fan and he has enjoyed two Channel 4 series in recent years, *Bank of Dave* and the follow-up *Bank of Dave: Fighting the Fat Cats.*

Former BBC TV weatherman John Kettley – who once had a novelty record called 'John Kettley is a Weatherman' by A Tribe of Toffs, which reached No. 21 in 1988 – is an ardent Clarets fan and has been known to mention his heroes in various forecasts and broadcasts over the years.

Alistair Campbell, one of the Clarets' most prominent supporters, was once the spin doctor for Prime Minister Tony Blair from 1997–2003, and he never missed a chance to let the nation know where his football loyalties lay.

Prince Charles – perhaps the most famous Clarets fan, even if it is only through affectionate reasons. His Royal Highness admitted his team was Burnley at a charity function in 2012, and we're happy to have him. Interestingly, Prince William also supports a team in claret and blue – Aston Villa. They must like a drop of claret at the Palace – Buckingham that is, not Crystal.

Jimmy Anderson, England's best fast bowler of the decade and the scourge of the Australians (until 2013 anyway), is a supporter, having been born in Burnley. The Lancashire paceman keeps tabs on his hometown club wherever he is in the world.

Sam Aston, who plays Chesney Brown in *Coronation Street*, is another Clarets fan. Aston has played the popular character since 2003.

BBC 5 Live breakfast presenter Tony Livesey, Burnley born and bred, is another famous supporter, as is *Emmerdale* actor Richard Moore, and the 'King of the Dingles', Zak (Steve Halliwell) has also been spotted at Turf Moor.

Shameless actress Alice Barry, who played Lillian Tyler from 2004 to 2013, is our final celebrity fan.

FAB FANS

The Beatles rarely associated themselves with football, even though their songs were regularly chanted by more than 20,000 Liverpool fans on the old Spion Kop. So one of the few football clubs to ever be associated with the Fab Four are Burnley, whose fans featured in The Beatles' movie *Help!* – along with Tottenham fans – as the crowds made their way to the 1962 FA Cup final. As the Clarets lost the game 3-1, it really was a hard day's night for the masses who trudged their way back to East Lancashire.

SEVEN CURIOUS FACTS ABOUT 'THE BEAST'

An American stunt pilot, Bryan Jensen, performed aerial acrobatics displays in his plane called 'The Beast' until 2011, when he sadly was killed during a show in Kansas. True fact, that.

While playing for Danish side B93's youth team, Jensen, then an outfield player, was asked to go in goal on the basis that he was the 'biggest and dumbest' guy in the squad – his words, not the author's!

While he was a free agent training with West Brom, Baggies' No. 1 commented that Jensen was 'nothing but a beast' when he answered questions on the Danish 'keeper.

In 2010, a biography of Jensen was released called (what else?) *The Beast – From Norrebro to the Premier League,* written by Danish writers Hans-Gerd Krabbe and Dan Hirsch Sorensen.

The Beast has an unusual middle name, Paldan, which has no meaning in English.

Jensen shares his nickname with Manchester City's Alvaro Negredo, Tottenham's Sandro, Fleetwood Town's Jon Parkin and former Arsenal striker Julio Baptista.

Jensen had a sausage named after him by a local Burnley butcher.

THE MANAGERS
NO. 13: HARRY POTTS, 1958–70

How fitting that Burnley's thirteenth manager should also prove the luckiest in the club's history. Harry Potts was yet another former Clarets player – a policy chairman Bob Lord firmly believed in – who was given the chance to bring the glory days back to Turf Moor.

Potts had made more than 150 appearances for Burnley between 1946 and 1950 before moving for big money, £20,000, to Everton, a well-trodden path for talented Clarets. Potts remained at Goodison Park for six years before retiring and moving into coaching.

He eventually took over as Shrewsbury Town manager, but barely two-thirds into the season, he got the call from Lord that he was never going to turn down. Potts inherited a squad with plenty of attacking flair and defensive nous – it seemed all that was missing was the right man to harness those strengths into a force to be reckoned with.

Billy Dougall's resignation and the uncertainty that had surrounded his tenure meant that Potts needed to quickly stamp his authority on the team, but with little experience of his own to draw from, it represented a gamble by Lord. As it was, Potts steadied the ship and began what would become a dynasty at Turf Moor.

Sixth place was secured and he followed that up with seventh in his first full season – just two points shy of a top three place. It was the club's twelfth successive campaign in the top flight, which was only one season short of equalling the club record for consecutive terms in the top division.

The 1959/60 season would prove perhaps the greatest in the club's history yet, as Potts, still a relative rookie to management, guided the Clarets to a second league championship in the most dramatic fashion. Burnley had never been lower than seventh all season, and spent much of it in the top three but had never topped the table. A good FA Cup run meant that the Clarets' season would end after everybody else's had and with one game to play, a victory would guarantee the title.

Burnley made the short trip to Manchester City's Maine Road backed by thousands of travelling fans and, in a nail-biting match, edged home 2-1 to spark wild celebrations in Manchester and back home in East Lancs. Potts ensured his name would go down in the history books. The next two seasons were solid again, finishing fourth in 1960/61 as well as getting the semi-finals of both the FA Cup and League Cup, and the quarter-finals of the European Cup. In 1961/62, the Clarets almost bagged the elusive league and FA Cup double, but a disastrous end to the season saw the long-time leaders win just one of the final ten games to fritter the title away, as well as losing the FA Cup final to Tottenham. Immortality had beckoned for the squad of 1961/62, but the chance slipped through their fingers.

Potts rallied his side to finish third again the following season, but the two years that followed ended in mid-table and Potts' decision to sell crowd idol Jimmy McIlroy in 1963 had seen his popularity dip to an all-time low, with supporters questioning how he could sell the club talisman.

Potts still fashioned a title challenge from his charges in 1965/66 with a third place finish. The club maintained its position as the team of the early to mid-1960s, but as the end of the decade approached, the Clarets were a model of consistency finishing fourteenth for four successive years. Potts' time was coming to an end, yet it was still a shock when, after thumping Nottingham Forest 5-0 in February 1970, Potts was relieved of his managerial duties and, as they say in football, moved upstairs, finally leaving his toothless role of general manager in 1972.

The club's most successful manager wasn't quite finished at Turf Moor, however.

PLEASE (DON'T) RELEASE ME…

When Leighton James was released at the end of the 1986/87 season, his hopes of becoming the eighteenth player to clock up 300 league appearances had ended agonisingly on 298. However, he was offered the position of reserve team boss with manager Brian Miller wisely electing to keep James' registration as a player live, just in case. When Peter Zalem picked up an injury in the 1-0 win over Swansea – James' boyhood heroes – the former Wales international stepped in and played in the 1-0 win over Tranmere before clocking up appearance number 300 with a 1-0 win over, fittingly, Welsh side Wrexham.

MILK TURNS SOUR FOR SPURS

When the Clarets were drawn away to mid-table Spurs in the Milk Cup fifth round, most people expected the current FA Cup holders to move into the last eight of the competition, easing past a Division Two Burnley side fighting to avoid the drop into the third tier. Spurs, containing Ricky Villa, Osvaldo Ardiles and Glenn Hoddle, took the lead and the floodgates were expected to swing wide open. But bizarrely, Graham Roberts put the ball past his own keeper tweice to give the Clarets a 2-1 lead, and then Billy Hamilton scored a brace to secure a remarkable 4-1 win at White Hart Lane.

US AND THEM

The Clarets ended a thirty-five-year jinx when Sean Dyche's men secured a 2-1 win at Ewood Park in March 2014. After failing to win any of the previous eleven meetings in League and FA Cup since 1979 – seven defeats and four draws – revenge was finally achieved in Blackburn's own backyard, with the Clarets edging closer still to promotion. The last victory had also been at Ewood, by a score of 2-1. Yet when Jordan Rhodes put Rovers ahead, then Ben Mee cleared off the line and Rhodes hit the post, it looked as though it would end in anything but an away win – until goals from Jason Shackell and Danny Ings scored in the final twenty minutes to send the travelling Clarets wild.

CITY SLICKER

Ben Mee first made his name as an upcoming centre-back with Manchester City, and was the captain of the City side that won the 2008 FA Youth Cup by beating Chelsea 4-2 on aggregate over two legs.

FOX DROUGHT

Between 1983 and 2007, games between Burnley and Leicester City were a veritable non entity of entertaining football. Of the ten league games played during that period, only one match ended with more than one goal being scored. The Clarets won four, scored six times and conceded just three times – eight of the ten games resulted in a Burnley clean sheet!

A TALE OF ONE CITY?

Despite the Clarets' wretched home record against Manchester City in recent times, Turf Moor clashes with Manchester United have been largely the opposite. Over the past fifty years (going back to 1963), the Clarets have lost just twice in eleven league meetings with the Reds. Compare that same period with games against City where Burnley have won just three of the thirteen league and Cup meetings with the Blues, losing eight times and conceding twenty-nine goals in the process. Ouch!

TO HULL AND BACK

Though there has been the occasional roar, most Hull fans would admit that the Clarets are something of a bogey side since 1992. There have been twenty meetings during that time with Burnley losing five, drawing one and winning fourteen – seven in succession at one point between 2009 and 2012 – and Tigers failed to find the net in nine of those twenty clashes. 'Grrrreat!'

THE MANAGERS
NO. 14: JIMMY ADAMSON, 1970–76

Bob Lord continued his policy of promoting from within when Harry Potts' twelve-year reign came to an end. Jimmy Adamson had been on the coaching staff at Turf Moor since 1964, and had waited patiently for a chance to manage the club he loved, and had made more than 400 appearances for between 1947 and 1964.

Rarely was the phrase 'one-club man' better served. His coaching ability had seen him as a prominent member of England's backroom staff at the 1962 World Cup, and the FA offered him the chance to manage England ahead of Alf Ramsey, but he turned down the offer. So not only had Lord employed a loyal Clarets man, he had, in effect, the man who could have led England to the 1966 World Cup.

It was no surprise to anyone when Jimmy Adamson became manager of Burnley. He'd been in waiting for a number of years after retiring from the playing side and becoming a coach at the club. If the chairman had been eager to give his former captain a chance in the hot seat, it was understandable and perhaps influenced his decision to relieve Potts of his position; no doubt the continued interest from other clubs bound to turn Adamson's head one day.

So Potts' trusted lieutenant took command, and after overseeing the final few months of the 1969/70 campaign, Adamson boldly predicted the Clarets would be the team of the '70s, but his tenure couldn't have started much worse as Burnley were relegated after his first full season in charge ending the club's proud twenty-four-year stay in the top flight.

Adamson had perhaps underestimated the glue with which Potts had held his declining team together, and the first season in the second tier was more about adjustment and rebuilding as he set about fashioning a team in his own image. In 1972/73, the Clarets reclaimed their top flight place by winning the Second Division title.

Sixth place and an FA Cup semi-final represented a more than decent return in 1973/74, but the team was perhaps punching above its weight and a tenth place finish the following year was more realistic.

Adamson's tenure would come to an end midway through his sixth season in charge. An FA Cup third round defeat to Blackpool on 3 January, coupled with the fact the Clarets were third bottom of Division One, was enough for Lord to pull the trigger and sack Adamson, ending three decades' worth of service.

FOREST FIRE

Clashes between the Clarets and Nottingham Forest make very interesting reading, with one fact shining through – neither side likes to travel to the other's ground. With justification, both teams consider the other to be something of a bogey team when they travel, but on their own patch, it's a different story. Beginning with the Clarets, at Turf Moor since 1960, Forest have won just four of their last twenty-eight visits – poor form by anyone's book and one of those games ended in an 8-0 win for Burnley. In contrast, and in almost a mirror image, during the same time span the Clarets have failed to come away from the City Ground with a victory on twenty-one of their last twenty-four trips to Nottingham. Maybe both teams should save the travelling and just accept a home win and an away defeat?

SHIRT SPONSORS

Clarets fans will tell you their feet are firmly grounded, no matter whether the club is languishing at the bottom of the fourth tier of English football with one game to go or having just beaten Manchester United in the Premier League – and the list of shirt sponsors below is proof of a club who have kept it real over the years. OK, no mega money deals with soft drinks companies, airlines or payday loan companies, but the list of shirt sponsors will be remembered affectionately by Clarets fans for the part they've played in the club's recent history.

Endsleigh remain the longest sponsors, with a decade of their name emblazoned across the shirts of Burnley players, whereas in 2000/01, there was no sponsor – unthinkable in today's brand aware black hole of income and commercialism. A favourite was Holland's Pies, 2007–09, how could it not be? Premier Range will have got their money's worth as the Clarets looked anything but challengers for a return to the Premier League in 2012. The next sponsor, given the money-rich environment of the Premier League, will invariably be the club's biggest to date.

Years	Sponsor
1982–83	Poco
1983–84	TSB (Bank)
1984–87	Multipart
1988–98	Endsleigh
1998–2000	P3 Computers
2000–01	None
2001–03	Lanway
2003–04	Vodka Kick (away games)
2004–07	Hunters Property Group
2007–09	Holland's Pies (pie manufacturer)
2009–10	Samuel Cooke and Co Ltd
2010–12	Fun88.com Sportsbook & Casino
2012–14	Premier Range
2012–14	Oak Furniture Land (back of shirts only)

MASCOT

Bertie Bee is the official Burnley mascot, though Brentford also have a mascot of the same name. Bertie, who dons the 1882 number on his shirt, once rugby tackled a streaker who invaded the pitch at Turf Moor, though he had an uneasy relationship with the awkwardly named club sponsor mascot, Stan the Pie Man, courtesy of Holland's Pies.

BURNLEY FC PLAYER OF THE YEAR AWARDS, 2003–14

Here are the men the Clarets fans have voted for over the past eleven years:

Year	Winner
2003	Gareth Taylor
2004	Robbie Blake
2005	Gary Cahill
2006	Jon Harley
2007	Wade Elliott
2008	Wade Elliott
2009	Graham Alexander
2010	Steven Fletcher
2011	Jay Rodriguez
2012	Kieran Trippier
2013	Lee Grant
2014	Sam Vokes

HOT SHOTS

The position of the top Clarets scorer is frankly up for grabs, should a prolific scorer join the club and remain for five or six seasons. Charlie Austin, 2011–13, could have been that man, with forty-five goals in just ninety appearances. Had he continued that ratio, he would have rocketed to second all-time in just three more seasons. Two players, Bob Kelly and Willie Irvine, didn't make their century yet scrape into the top ten. George Beel's 187 goals came in just nine years at Turf Moor. He reached double figures in all nine seasons he played and is also the club's top league goals scorer, and achieved the feat in just 337 games.

Name	Years	Goals (all comps)
George Beel	1923–32	187
Ray Pointer	1957–65	132
Jimmy McIlroy	1950–63	131
Andy Lochhead	1960–68	128
Louis Page	1925–31	115
Bert Freeman	1911–21	115
John Connelly	1956–64	104
Jimmy Robson	1956–65	100
Bob Kelly	1913–25	97
Willie Irvine	1960–68	97

THE MANAGERS
NO.15: JOE BROWN, 1976/77

Bod Lord, true to his beliefs, promoted yet again from his coaching staff when Jimmy Adamson was shown the door at the start of 1976. Joe Brown, from the Turf Moor backroom staff, succeeded the outgoing manager, but Brown's stay was to be short-lived.

Universally liked as a man, Brown perhaps lacked the killer instinct to survive in the shark-infested waters of management. A former Burnley player whose career was ended by a serious back injury, Brown had spent fifteen years as a coach and guided the Clarets to their only FA Youth Cup success in 1968.

There were clear factions in the dressing room who disagreed with Adamson's sacking, and unfortunately it showed on the pitch. The Clarets were relegated at the end of the season, having lost ten of Brown's first seventeen games in charge. With just four wins in twenty-four league games the following season, the club were in danger of successive demotions. After just thirteen months in the job, Brown was axed as a depressingly familiar pattern at Turf Moor had begun to emerge.

MASTERS AND SERVANTS

Here are the top ten players who have appeared for the Clarets since the formation of the club. Jerry Dawson's twenty-two-year career at Turf Moor ensures he will be tough to shift at the top of the tree, while Alan Stevenson clocked up the most appearances in the least amount of time, with 543 games in just eleven years. Leighton James' three spells at Turf Moor sees him creep into the top ten, and Martin Dobson's two spells see him up to fifth. In today's merry-go-round of transfer activity, it may be some time – if at all – before this particular list is breached.

Name	Years	Apps (all comps)
Jerry Dawson	1907–29	569
Alan Stevenson	1972–83	543
John Angus	1955–72	521
Jimmy McIlroy	1950–63	497
Martin Dobson	1967–74, 1979–1984	497
Jimmy Adamson	1950–1964	486
Tommy Cummings	1947–1963	479
Brian Miller	1955–1966	455
Fred Barron	1898–1911	423
Leighton James	1970–75, 78–80 & 86–89	399

FIRST OUT OF THE BLOCKS

The 1993/94 season was particularly profitable for the Clarets in terms of racing out of the blocks first, with no less than five goals inside the first minute. Adrian Heath's twelve-second goal against Blackpool in the Marsden Cup got the campaign off to a flyer, and Kevin Russell bagged one after thirty-six seconds against Brighton at

Turf Moor. The Seagulls were also on the receiving end in the clash at the Goldstone Ground as Steve Davis powered home a header after fifty-five seconds. David Eyre bagged one a fraction earlier, after fifty-four seconds at Cambridge. Three of the games ended in a win, with only the away trip to Brighton ending in a 1-1 draw. Impressively, the Clarets bagged eleven goals inside the first ten minutes in all competitions, and nine of those games ended in victory.

MARSDEN CUP OF WOE

In the days before glitzy pre-season tours, the Clarets were happy to take part in the Marsden Lancashire Cup, a useful enough pre-season tournament and one that, in July 1993, ticked a lot of boxes.

Starting against Blackpool, Adrian Heat gave a new-look Burnley side the lead after just twelve seconds, but the Seasiders fought back to lead 2-1 until substitute Mick Conroy scored twice to give the Clarets an exciting 3-2 win, and impressive start to the campaign. Three days later, Bolton left Turf Moor with a 1-0 win after seventy-eighth-minute goal, meaning that only a victory by a four-goal margin at Rochdale would see Jimmy Mullen's men into the final, but instead Dale walloped the Clarets 4-1 to end hopes of an early piece of silverware. Ah, well.

THE ULTIMATE UTILITY MAN?

With 329 appearances in all competitions between 1987 and 1994, Andy Farrell can probably – and justifiably – claim to be the ultimate utility man for the Clarets. In a time when the shirt numbers went from 1 to 14 and only two subs were allowed, Farrell wore every single shirt during his time at Turf Moor. Though he began in the No. 8 jersey on his Burnley debut, he proceeded to go through the numbers in the following order: 8, 7, 2, 4, 3, 14, 10, 11, 5, 12, 1, 6, 9. He donned the 'keeper's jersey against Stockport County in January 1991, when Chris Pearce was sent off after just nine minutes. During his eighty-one minutes, plus injury time, between the sticks, he helped his team to a 3-2 victory. He completed the set during a 2-1 win over Preston North End in August 1993 – almost exactly six years since his debut – and in doing so wrote his name into the club's history books by becoming the first player to achieve the feat.

THE MANAGERS
NO.16: HARRY POTTS, 1977–79

Harry Potts had returned to Burnley in the role of chief scout during Joe Brown's tenure. For Bob Lord, turning to Potts to save the Clarets from a crisis and Third Division football seemed the most logical thing to do.

He had had been in charge of Blackpool for a spell and even oversaw the FA Cup win over the Clarets, that cost Jimmy Adamson his job. Potts stopped the rot and ensured second tier football for another season, but with a weakened squad following sales of several influential players, Burnley started the 1977/78 campaign disastrously, and went into the new year bottom of Division Two – but just three defeats in the final nineteen games saw Potts' side climb well clear of the drop.

Potts still was able to conjure the old magic every now and then, and while the Anglo-Scottish Cup may not have been worthy of an open-top bus tour around town, it was a morale-booster nonetheless and started the 1978/79 campaign with a bang. But it was merely a stay of execution for Harry, as his team ended the season without a win in eight and started the new campaign without a win in sixteen – a record run of twenty-four matches in total. Needless to say Potts' reign was soon over at Turf Moor. It was a sad end for a man who had done more for Burnley Football Club than perhaps anybody else.

INTERNATIONAL CAPS

Players who have won international caps while with Burnley are as follows:

ALBANIA: Besart Berisha
CAMEROON: Andre Amougou
CANADA: David Edgar
ENGLAND: John Angus/William Bannister/Tommy Boyle/Jack Bruton/Ralph Coates/John Connelly/James Crabtree/Jerry Dawson/ Martin Dobson/Billy Elliott/Bert Freeman/Gordon Harris/Jack Hill/Jack Hillman/Bob Kelly/Colin McDonald/Brian Miller/ Eddie Mosscrop/Louis Page/Brian Pilkington/Ray Pointer/George Waterfield/Willie Watson/Jack Yates
GREECE: Nik Michopoulos/Dimi Papadopoulos
GUYANA: Leon Cort
ICELAND: Joey Gudjonsson
NORTHERN IRELAND: Tommy Cassidy/Terry Cochrane/ Michael Duff/Alex Elder/William Emerson/Hugh Flack/Phil Gray/Billy Hamilton/Willie Irvine/Steve Jones/Danny Lafferty/Kyle Lafferty/ Andy McCluggage/Jimmy McIlroy/Tom Morrison/Martin Paterson/ Sammy Todd/Tom Willighan
REPUBLIC OF IRELAND: Keith Treacy
JAMAICA: Micah Hyde/Dane Richards
NEW ZEALAND: Cameron Howieson
SCOTLAND: Jock Aird/Graham Alexander/Adam Blacklaw/Steven Caldwell/Steven Fletcher/Chris Iwelumo/Willie Morgan
TRINIDAD & TOBAGO: Ian Cox
WALES: Stan Bowsher/Danny Coyne/Brian Flynn/Leighton James/ Billy Morris/Gareth Taylor/Sam Vokes

OUTSTAYING HIS WELCOME?

In the 6 December 1986 matchday programme against Manchester United, the Clarets 'A Warm Welcome to' section said, 'Congratulations to Alex Ferguson on his appointment as Manchester United manager. We wish him the best of luck in the job, in which he is assisted by Archie Knox, formerly his No. 2 at Aberdeen.' Little did we know what lay ahead. The programme, incidentally, carried just five pages of editorial in its twenty-four-page format and cost 50p. Well, you get what you pay for.

MORECAMBE LIGHTS

The Clarets accepted an invitation to help Morecambe celebrate the installation of their new floodlights on 4 August 1993. The hosts, in the HFS Loans Premier Division, were up for the occasion, and secured a 2-1 win over a strong Burnley side with Adrian Heath's goal counting for little on the day.

WEMBLEY BECKONS

The Football League Trophy 1987/88, known briefly as the Sherpa Van Trophy 1987/88 (for sponsorship reasons), was the fifth staging of the knockout competition for English football clubs in the Third and Fourth Divisions (now known as League One and Two).

The competition began on 13 October 1987, and ended with the final on 29 May 1988. The tournament began with clubs divided into a Northern and a Southern section, and teams entering a preliminary group stage. Each section then gradually eliminated the qualifying teams in knockout fashion until each had a winning finalist. The two winning finalists then faced each other in the combined final for the honour of the trophy.

The Clarets had reached the Freight Rover Trophy final in 1988. The Wolves were the opposition in the final at Wembley, and it was the first time in the competition's history that two former English champions had faced each other in the final. This is Burnley got there:

Northern Section
Group 1
Rochdale 0–0 Tranmere Rovers

Tranmere Rovers　　1–2　　Burnley
　　　　　　　　　　　　　　Oghani 4
　　　　　　　　　　　　　　Grewcock 68
Att: 1,801

Burnley　3–2　　Rochdale
　　　　　　　　Grewcock 7
　　　　　　　　Reeves 43
　　　　　　　　Farrell 77
Att: 2,677

	P	W	D	L	F	A	Pts	GD
Burnley	2	2	0	0	5	3	6	+3
Rochdale	2	0	1	1	2	3	1	-1
Tranmere R	2	0	1	1	1	2	1	-1

Burnley　1-0　　Chester
　　　　　　　　Oghani 80
Att: 3,436

Quarter-final:
Bury　0-1　Burnley
　　　　　Comstive 37 (pen)

Semi-final:
Burnley   0-0   Halifax (Burnley win 5-3 on pens)
Att: 10,222

Northern Area Final
First Leg:
Burnley   0–0   Preston North End
Attendance: 15,680

Preston North End   1–3   Burnley (Burnley win 3-1 on aggregate)
Oghani 32
Hoskin 93
Comstive 117

Att: 17,592

Final
29 May 1988
Burnley   0–2   Wolverhampton Wanderers
Mutch 22, Dennison 51

EUROPEAN CUP

The Clarets' 1959/60 Division One title meant the club qualified for European competition for the first time. With the European Cup in its infancy – this was only the fifth year it had been held – Burnley were drawn against French champions Stade de Reims, with the first leg at Turf Moor ending in a 2-0 win for the Clarets. The second leg proved an exciting affair, but Burnley did just enough, losing 3-2 but progressing through on aggregate 4-3.

With only sixteen teams competing, that meant Burnley were already in the quarter-finals, and a thrilling 3-1 win over SV Hamburg at Turf Moor, meant a solid away performance would put the Clarets within reach of the final. But the Germans were far from finished and won the return leg 4-1 at the Volkparkstadion to send Burnley spiralling out 5-4 on aggregate. It had been an exhilarating ride, but it was over and it was the one and only time the club has competed in Europe's Premier Club competition, now known as the Champions League, of course.

THE MANAGERS
NO. 17: BRIAN MILLER, 1977–83

Brian Miller followed a well-trodden path from coaching staff to management at Turf Moor, but inherited a wretched situation from previous boss Harry Potts. Bottom of Division Two, the former Clarets skipper couldn't reverse what had become inevitable relegation to the third tier for the first time in the club's history.

Miller's first full season didn't end in the promotion the supporters had hoped for, but the 1981/82 season did – despite being bottom in October – with the Clarets crowned Division Three champions, after pipping Carlisle United on goal difference.

Miller's hopes of strengthening the team with several upcoming players, rumoured to be Peter Reid and John Aldridge, were dashed, and instead Burnley were relegated back to the third tier at the first time of asking – a yoyo culture had enveloped Turf Moor and Miller left halfway through the 1983/84 campaign with promotion looking a distant dream.

INTER-CITY FAIRS CUP

Finishing third place in Division One in 1965/66 meant Burnley qualified for European competition for the second time in six years. This time it was the Inter-City Fairs Cup, later known as the UEFA Cup, and eventually the Europa League. The Clarets qualified along with Leeds United and West Brom.

The first round saw Burnley draw VfB Stuttgart, and after securing a 1-1 draw in Germany, the Clarets won the home leg 2-0 to progress 3-1 on aggregate, drawing Swiss side FC Lausanne-Sport. This was anything but a straightforward tie, with the Swiss outfit winning the first leg 3-1. It meant that the Clarets needed a huge performance in the second leg, and that's exactly what happened, with a thumping 5-0 seeing the Lancastrians comfortably through 6-3 on aggregate, as well as maintaining a 100 per cent record in Europe at Turf Moor.

The third round threw up Italian opposition in the form of Napoli, but Burnley were in irresistible form at Turf Moor and took a healthy lead of 3-0 back to Naples. The Clarets then survived some rough house tactics from the hosts to draw 0-0, and reach the quarter-finals of a European competition for the second time in succession. Yet again they faced German opposition in Eintracht Frankfurt, and yet again the Clarets were eliminated at this stage, drawing 1-1 at Turf Moor before narrowly losing 2-1 in Germany.

In 2010/11, Burnley were in with a chance of a shock Europa League spot via the Fair Play League, with all the clubs above the Clarets having already qualified. But England dropped from third to seventh in the FIFA World Rankings list and weren't offered an extra place in Europe.

CLARETS BOOKS

Here are some recommended reads on Burnley FC:

Laws of the Jungle by Brian Laws with Alan Briggs
Thanks for the Memories by Roger Eli with Dave Thomas
Tommy Boyle – A Story Worth Telling by Mike Smith
Entertainment, Heroes and Villains by Dave Thomas
Images of Sport – Burnley Football Club by Ray Simpson
Heroes of Winter by Mike Prestage
Big Club, Small Town and Me by Brendan Flood
The Burnley Miscellany by David Wiseman

ANYONE FOR TENNIS?

Back in 1975, Wimbledon was only associated with one thing – tennis. But in 1975, the football club of the same name really made their mark as they put Burnley on a list nobody wants to end up on; the top FA Cup shocks of all time. The Clarets, then in the First Division, had drawn the Dons out of the hat, and nothing other than a comfortable home win was expected.

The visitors had barely started their remarkable journey from the Southern League to the top flight, but were already causing something of a stir due to their in your face attitude. They were determined to head back south with something, and from the early exchanges it was clear that the hosts were in for a feisty ninety minutes.

Micky Mahon scored for Wimbledon and the Clarets spent the rest of the game trying to put the ball past Dicky Guy, who made a string of magnificent saves to preserve his side's slender advantage and he was the difference between the teams on the day.

For the Clarets, they became the first top flight side to lose to a non-league outfit since 1920, but for Wimbledon, who had already navigated six rounds to get to that stage, it was just the beginning of an amazing journey, and they were rewarded with a trip to League champions Leeds United in round four, where they pulled off perhaps an even more stunning 0-0 draw, before eventually succumbing in the replay at Plough Lane.

THE MANAGERS
NO. 18: FRANK CASPER, 1983

Brian Miller had been sacked on the eve of a crucial Milk Cup quarter-final away to Tottenham. It was a game nobody gave the Clarets a cat in hell's chance of winning, so when Frank Casper stepped up from a coaching role to take command, it looked little else than a fool's errand. But Burnley turned in a superb display at White Hart Lane, beating a star-studded Spurs 4-1 and earning Casper the job on a permanent basis. Despite a valiant effort, he couldn't prevent relegation to Division Three and the Milk Cup adventure ended at the semi-final stage. The manner of the final-day defeat to Crystal Palace, which kept the Eagles up and sent the Clarets down, did the most damage to Casper's reputation as a manager. After his dismissal, chairman John Jackson revealed that, for the first time in twenty-seven years, the club would not be employing from within when seeking a replacement.

THEY DON'T WRITE 'EM LIKE
THAT ANYMORE

The *Burnley Gazette's* report from a 1909 reserve game is hereby repeated in full – the words, the phrases and the writing shows exactly how it was way back when – and makes for an entertaining read.

Saturday, 16 January 1909

Reserves, Lancashire Combination, Turf Moor
Burnley Reserves 4-1 Liverpool Reserves
Attendance: 5,000

Burnley Reserves (2-3-5): Jack Hillman; William Howarth, Harry Woodward; Stephen Heys, Rupert Cawthorne, Fred Minion; John Beddow, Dick Lindley, Robert Brewis, Tommy Mayson, Arthur Dawson.

Liverpool Reserves (2-3-5): Don Sloan; George Latham, Percy Saul; Messina Allman, Ernest Peake, Sam Hignett; Harold Uren, Bertram Goode, William Hunter, Sam Bowyer, Mike Griffin.

Thunder and lightning, and a strong blizzard, formed the setting to one of the most exhilarating games seen at Turf Moor this season, when Burnley Reserves met and right well defeated the Liverpool Reserves.

Notwithstanding the fact that the ground was heavy with the recent rains and snows, the Burnley men just seemed to delight in it and the way they ploughed through was a treat. If one man stood out above another it was Beddow, who has lately developed a turn of speed and resource which are worthy of the first team. Perhaps he was not far ahead of Minion in usefulness, for the latter undoubtedly gave a fine exhibition. The right wing was much better than the left. Lindley co-operating grandly with Beddow, while on the other side the play was of too individuals nature, Mayson being the bigger offender, and some of his brilliant pieces of play did not have the effect they should have had on this account. Brewis showed a good deal of improvement at entre. The half-way line was strong all through. Minion and Cawthorne taking the foremost rank. Howarth, especially in the second half, was not capable of holding the extreme winger, and Woodward was if anything the better of the backs, though if the shooting of Liverpool had been anything like accurate the result might have been more nearly level. Hillman had not the amount of work to do that Sloan had, and was obviously at fault when he let the Liverpool goal through. He evidently thought it was going over, and he made no effort to ensure that it did so.

Burnley had the wind against them in the first half, and a strong wind it was. If anything they had the most of the play, though Liverpool assisted by the breeze, were repeatedly dangerous Hillman brought off one or two good saves, the wind making the ball extremely tricky. On one occasion Goode had got through and when right in front of goal was steadying himself for the shot, but Minion dashed in and just diverted the shot beyond the post. Soon after this Mayson broke away and, beating Hignett, dashed for goal, but when close in he lost control and Brewis, getting the leather, shot into Sloan's hands.

Some grand work by Lindley and Beddow resulted in the latter putting in a smart shot. With the game twenty minutes old, Goode put in a hard shot right over Hillman's head. The ball struck the crossbar and rebounded into the net. Despite the heavy wind, Burnley played up well, but had bad luck till just before half-time when a good shot by Beddow went into the net off one of the visitors' backs.

Half-time Burnley Reserves, 1 Liverpool Reserves 1.

A dangerous movement by Liverpool was made in the first minute of the second half, but bad shooting characterised the finish. A minute later the ball was taken to the other end, and from Beddow's pass Lindley shot, the ball entering the net off Hunter, who tried to head behind. The game continued to be well contested, but Burnley were much superior in shooting. After a brief stoppage owing to a heavy hail storm, the game was resumed at hot pressure. Dawson put in a beautiful centre, which Brewis almost converted. Lindley ended a brilliant effort by beating Sloan for the third time, and after Beddow had forced his way through half-a-dozen players Mayson scored the fourth goal to secure a 4-1 win.

HOW TIMES CHANGE

Transfer records are only as good as the latest big-money deal, but the Clarets' current incoming and outgoing records, both involving Steven Fletcher, had stood for several years going into July 2014. The highest fee paid was £3 million for Fletcher from Hibs in 2008, and a year later he was on his way to Wolves for a record fee paid of £7 million. No doubt, these records will soon be replaced by new ones. Looking back to the pre-war record, James Clayton was the record buy at £3,500 in 1938. Clayton swapped one claret and blue (Aston Villa) for those of Burnley, and the highest pre-war fee received was Jack Hill, who left for Newcastle in 1928 for the princely sum of £8,000.

THE MANAGERS
NO. 19: JOHN BOND, 1983/84

Burnley's first external managerial recruitment since 1956 proved an unmitigated disaster for all concerned. Former Manchester City boss John Bond was signed on in what was something of a coup for the Clarets. The announcement the larger than life Bond was taking over at Turf Moor pumped much-needed life into the club, as did some of Bond's early signings, which included the graceful former City and Scotland winger Tommy Hutchison and former £1 million England striker Kevin Reeves.

There was uneasiness about his decision to replace the majority of the Clarets' backroom staff, but his team, inspired by the influential Reeves, played some good football, and as late as February looked well-placed for promotion. But injury to Reeves saw the challenge fritter away and the absence of Bond for a number of games – said to be away scouting new players – saw the tide slowly begin to turn against the manager.

Bond brought in many ageing, free transfers during the summer before a very public fall-out with the board. Just days before the new season was about to begin, Bond was sacked. In later years, the flamboyant manager admitted he made a lot of mistakes during his year or so in East Lancashire, with the decision to discard so many respected members of the backroom staff perhaps his biggest error. Relying on too many trusted lieutenants who had served well elsewhere – mostly City – was also an error of judgement, though understandable that he should turn to experienced former internationals who he though could still do a job. He left behind big wages attached to ageing legs and Bond, who moved on to Swansea, is not fondly remembered as the club slipped into its darkest period yet with relegation to the Fourth Division at the end of the 1984/85 campaign. Some supporters still blame Bond for the club very nearly slipping out of the league altogether.

DENNIS THE MENACE

Dennis Tueart – scorer of that League final winning goal in 1976 – arrived at Turf Moor at the wrong end of an illustrious career. Aged thirty-four when he arrived on a free from Stoke City, the former Manchester City, Sunderland, New York Cosmos and England forward, agreed to join John Bond in late December 1983. He got off to a flier, too, scoring on his debut during a 5-0 win over Scunthorpe United to instantly win over any doubters. The remainder of his half-season in claret and blue was mainly from the bench as he started nine times and came on as sub on a further ten occasions. He managed another four goals to make a decent statistic of four goals from nine starts, but his game time was limited towards the end of the campaign, and he also had the disadvantage of being labelled a 'Bond man', which, at the time, didn't help matters. Tueart left for Derry City after just six months at Turf Moor.

PLAY-OFFS

2009 Championship Play-off

The Clarets have featured in the play-offs on two occasions. The 2009 Championship play-off saw Burnley facing Sheffield United for a place in the Premier League. Dubbed one of the most important club football games anywhere in the world, because of the television money the Premier League offered, the Clarets were looking to end a thirty-three-year wait to return to the top flight against a Sheffield United side managed by Kevin Blackwell. The only goal for Owen Coyle's talented side came on thirteen minutes, when Wade Elliot's sumptuous curling shot was enough to win the game. Blades were reduced to ten men when substitute Ward was sent off after eighty minutes, and Lee Hendrie was also red carded after the final whistle on a miserable afternoon for the South Yorkshire side. For

Graham Alexander, it also ended a play-off jinx with his first win in seven attempts.

Burnley: Jensen, Duff, Carlisle, Caldwell, Kalvenes, Elliott, Alexander, McCann (Gudjonsson 27), Blake (Eagles 69), Thompson (Rodriguez 73), Paterson. Subs Not Used: Penny, McDonald. Booked: Carlisle, Kalvenes.

Sheff Utd: Kenny, Walker, Morgan, Kilgallon, Naughton, Montgomery, Howard (Lupoli 82), Cotterill (Ward 58), Stephen Quinn (Hendrie 85), Halford, Beattie. Subs Not Used: Bennett, Bromby. Sent Off: Ward (80) Booked: Ward, Lupoli.
Att: 80,518

1994 Second Division Play-off
The Clarets had a nervy ride to the 1993/94 play-off final at Wembley after a tense semi-final against Plymouth Argyle. Argyle had finished third while the Clarets had finished sixth, and when the teams met at Turf Moor for the first leg, it was the Devon side who seemed to have the advantage after a 0-0 draw in front of 18,794 fans. Things looked even worse when Plymouth went ahead after fifteen minutes of the second leg at Home Park, but two goals in two minutes from John Francis tipped the tie the Clarets' way, and a third from Warren Joyce booked a place at Wembley against Stockport County. It was interesting to note that both Plymouth and Stockport has been in second spot in the final days of the season before being pipped by Port Vale at the post. A crowd of almost 45,000 watched the two north-west teams play for a place in the second tier of English football. County struck first, with Chris Beaumont scoring after just two minutes. But David Eyres equalised just before the half-hour mark, and Gary Parkinson's second-half winner was enough to send Burnley up.
Att: 44,806

THE MANAGERS
NOS 20 TO 34, 1984–2014

After John Bond's departure in 1984, fifteen more managers filled the Turf Moor hot-seat over next thirty years, with each one, on average, lasting two years:

John Benson – August 1984 to May 1985
Martin Buchan – June 1985 to October 1985
Tommy Cavanagh – October 1985 to May 1986
Brian Miller – July 1986 to January 1989
Frank Casper – January 1989 to October 1991
Jimmy Mullen – October 1991 to February 1996
Clive Middlemass – February 1996 to March 1996
Adrian Heath – March 1996 to June 1997
Chris Waddle – July 1997 to May 1998
Stan Ternent – June 1998 to May 2004
Steve Cotterill – June 2004 to November 2007
Owen Coyle – November 2007 to January 2010
Brian Laws – January 2010 to December 2010
Eddie Howe – January 2011 to October 2012
Sean Dyche – October 2012 – present (up to 1 July 2014)

WALES WATCHING

The fortieth Home Internationals Championships saw Burnley host England for the first and only time on 28 November 1927. It was a proud moment for Clarets skipper Jack Hill, but it proved to be memorable for all the wrong reasons. A Turf Moor crowd of 32,089 eagerly awaited the two teams.

England had already lost their opening match to Ireland and knew nothing less than a victory over the Welsh would do. But when Hill put through his own goal as Wales went on to win 2-1, England would end bottom of the group with Wales topping the table. No wonder there were no more internationals at the Turf. That said, England Women, England under-21s, England under-20s and England B have all staged games at Burnley in later years.

FLOODLIGHTS

Turf Moor's floodlights were switched on for the first time when the Clarets hosted a friendly with Blackburn Rovers on 16 December 1957.

GUNNER BE ANOTHER DEFEAT?

From September 1927 to March 1954, Arsenal were very much the Clarets' bogey team at Turf Moor. The Gunners failed to lose a single game at Burnley for twenty-seven years, winning four and drawing five of the nine matches played, scoring twelve goals and conceding eight.

FA YOUTH CUP 1968

Burnley won the FA Youth Cup for the first and only time in season 1967/68. The Clarets played Coventry City at Highfield Road in the first leg, losing 2-1, but the youngsters turned the tie around at Turf Moor, winning 2-0 and 3-2 overall on aggregate to lift the coveted under-18s competition trophy. Notable names included skipper Mick Docherty, Steve Kindon and Dave Thomas.

The team that played over two legs was: Gerry McEvoy, Peter Jones, Mick Docherty (captain), Wilf Wrigley, Eddie Cliff, Eric Probert, Alan West, Dave Hartley, Willie Brown, Dave Thomas, Steve Kindon Sub: George Coppock.

ORIENT EXPRESS

For a match, occasion or moment known to the majority of Burnley fans as 'The Orient Game', few matches in the club's history can match the magnitude of a game that many believe could have been the end of line, had things gone wrong. The scenario was simple – the Clarets had to win their final game of the season to stay in the League and then hope Lincoln City slipped up in their match. Burnley had been in decline for many years, so to be rock bottom of the Fourth Division with one game to go suggested there was a certain inevitability about the Clarets' demotion to non-League football.

A crowd approaching 18,000 packed into Turf Moor for a game that was equally important to Orient, who still harboured hopes of making the play-offs and had already won the first encounter of the season 2-0 at Brisbane Road. With the kick-off delayed to allow everyone who wanted to get in time to filter into the stadium, the Clarets already had the advantage of knowing that there would be at least fifteen minutes at the end when their fate would be known, and perhaps there would be an opportunity to do something about it.

From the kick-off, it was clear that Burnley were up for the game and Orient looked a little unsettled in such a red-hot atmosphere; their early exchanges were littered with mistakes and meaty challenges. As the game edged towards the break goalless, the goal the home fans had been willing finally came as Neil Grewcock beat three defenders before hammering the ball past 'keeper David Cass, to send Turf Moor wild. Three minutes after the break and Grewcock was this time the provider as his free-kick found the head of Ian Britton, who nodded past Cass, and gave the Clarets much-needed breathing space.

Alan Comfort pulled one back for Orient eight minutes later to ensure nails were bitten to the last kick of the game, but the Clarets clung on and with news Lincoln had lost their game, survival was confirmed and celebrated with an obligatory pitch invasion.

One thing was for sure; the fans and players knew that this famous old club could never be allowed to slip so close to the trapdoor ever again. Lessons were learned and, over time, acted upon.

Burnley's team that day was: Neenan, Leebrook, Hampton, Rodaway, Gallagher, Deakin, Grewcock, Malley, James 6, Devaney, Britton.
Referee: G Courtney (Spennymoor).
Attendance: 17,600
The Fourth Division final table 1986/87 (see opposite):

Pos	Team	P	W	D	L	F	A	W	D	L	F	A	F	A	GD	Pts
1	Northampton Town	46	20	2	1	56	20	10	7	6	47	33	103	53	+50	99
2	Preston North End	46	16	4	3	36	18	10	8	5	36	29	72	47	+25	90
3	Southend United	46	14	4	5	43	27	11	1	11	25	28	68	55	+13	80
4	Wolves	46	12	3	8	36	24	12	4	7	33	26	69	50	+19	79
5	Colchester United	46	15	3	5	41	20	6	4	13	23	36	64	56	+8	70
6	Aldershot	46	13	5	5	40	22	7	5	11	24	35	64	57	+7	70
7	Orient	46	15	2	6	40	25	5	7	11	24	36	64	61	+3	69
8	Scunthorpe United	46	15	3	5	52	27	3	9	11	21	30	73	57	+16	66
9	Wrexham	46	8	13	2	38	24	7	7	9	32	27	70	51	+19	65
10	Peterborough United	46	10	7	6	29	21	7	7	9	28	29	57	50	+7	65
11	Cambridge United	46	12	6	5	37	23	5	5	13	23	39	60	62	-2	62
12	Swansea City	46	13	3	7	31	21	4	8	11	25	40	56	61	-5	62
13	Cardiff City	46	6	12	5	24	18	9	4	10	24	32	48	50	-2	61
14	Exeter City	46	11	10	2	37	17	0	13	10	16	32	53	49	+4	56
15	Halifax Town	46	10	5	8	32	32	5	5	13	27	42	59	74	-15	55
16	Hereford United	46	10	6	7	33	23	4	5	14	27	38	60	61	-1	53
17	Crewe Alexandra	46	8	9	6	38	35	5	5	13	32	37	70	72	-2	53
18	Hartlepool United	46	6	11	6	24	30	5	7	11	20	35	44	65	-21	51
19	Stockport County	46	9	6	8	25	27	4	6	13	15	42	40	69	-29	51
20	Tranmere Rovers	46	6	10	7	32	37	5	7	11	22	35	54	72	-18	50
21	Rochdale	46	6	8	7	31	30	3	9	11	23	43	54	73	-19	50
22	Burnley	46	9	7	7	31	35	3	6	14	22	39	53	74	-21	49
23	Torquay United	46	8	8	7	28	29	2	10	11	28	43	56	72	-16	48
24	Lincoln City	46	8	7	8	30	27	4	5	14	15	38	45	65	-20	48

THE MILLION POUND MAN

Ian Moore became Burnley's first £1 million signing when he moved to Turf Moor in 2000. Moore, son of former Tranmere boss Ronnie Moore, had been impressing Stockport County, for whom he'd also been a record big-money signing. Moore, then aged twenty-four, had found goals hard to come by during his career, with just thirty-three goals in more than 170 games, but his all-round work rate and commitment to the team quickly made him a favourite at Turf Moor. His speed and determination embodied a spirit drawn from the terraces, and his 'never say die' attitude became a trademark of his game. But as his career progressed, he was switched more to the wing and he seemed to suffer a dip in form. A nasty injury then saw him return without much of the pace that had been such a huge part of his game. After five years with the Clarets, and having played more than 200 games, Moore left for Leeds United in 2005 for a knock-down £50,000 and later played for Hartlepool, Tranmere and Rotherham United. On marrying in 2009, Moore took the surname of his wife to become Ian Thomas-Moore, and retired as a played in 2013.

BEER MAT FACTS

So you are asked in the pub, 'What's so special about Burnley?' and you need a quick response, just rattle off these ten facts and you'll impress friends, family and strangers alike.

1) Burnley are one of only three teams to have won all four divisional titles, along with Wolves and Preston.
2) Only Preston North End have occupied the same ground for longer than Burnley, who moved into Turf Moor in 1883.

3) Only a last-day win over Leyton Orient, as recently as 1987, saved Burnley from becoming the first of the Football League's twelve founders since Accrington to drop out of the league.

4) Burnley only adopted their famous claret and blue strip in 1910, paying homage to the great Aston Villa side of the day. Prior to that, they had turned out in a selection of kits, ranging from green, to black and amber.

5) The last time the title headed to Turf Moor, Burnley got their timing exactly right. They went top for the first time in the campaign on the last day of the season, after beating Manchester City 2-1 to claim the championship.

6) Burnley's thirty-match unbeaten run in 1921 stood as the longest stretch without defeat in league history until Arsenal bettered it – managing a whole season without loss – in 2003/04.

7) The 1956 FA Cup fourth-round tie with Chelsea is one of the longest in history as the pair drew 1-1 twice, then 0-0, the 2-2, before a 2-0 Chelsea win in the fifth game finally settled it.

8) Burnley have won every major competition in English football, except the League Cup.

9) Jack Yeats became Burnley's first ever international in 1889, and even managed two goals on his debut, yet he never played another game for England.

10) Turf Moor will be expanded to 28,000 to cope with Premier League football, but it's not a patch on the record 54,775 who turned out to watch an FA Cup tie with Huddersfield in 1924.

STATS AND FACTS SECTION

Here you'll find records, stats and obscure competitions – all in one handy place.

CLARETS V. ROVERS

THE COMPLETE RECORD

There's no love lost between the Clarets and Blackburn Rovers, but despite the hostility, each would miss the other if they no longer existed. Derby day, the banter, songs and passion – the fixture may not happen every season, but when it does, the fire and brimstone of the East Lancashire can match that of any major derby in the world. The Clarets, at long last, became top dogs in the area for the first time in three decade when promotion was secured in 2013/14. Here we trace every single meeting for easy perusal.

Complete record: Won 36, Drawn 18, Lost 41

Date	Match	Score	Competition
03 Nov 1888	Burnley *v.* Blackburn Rovers	1-7	Division One
04 Feb 1889	Blackburn Rovers *v.* Burnley	4-2	Division One
26 Oct 1889	Blackburn Rovers *v.* Burnley	7-1	Division One
22 Feb 1890	Burnley *v.* Blackburn Rovers	1-2	Division One
18 Oct 1890	Burnley *v.* Blackburn Rovers	1-6	Division One
22 Nov 1890	Blackburn Rovers *v.* Burnley	5-2	Division One
26 Sep 1891	Blackburn Rovers *v.* Burnley	3-3	Division One
12 Dec 1891	Burnley *v.* Blackburn Rovers	3-0	Division One
03 Dec 1892	Burnley *v.* Blackburn Rovers	0-0	Division One
17 Dec 1892	Blackburn Rovers *v.* Burnley	2-0	Division One
18 Nov 1893	Blackburn Rovers *v.* Burnley	3-2	Division One
23 Dec 1893	Burnley *v.* Blackburn Rovers	1-0	Division One

17 Nov 1894	Blackburn Rovers *v.* Burnley	1-0	Division One
12 Jan 1895	Burnley *v.* Blackburn Rovers	2-1	Division One
05 Oct 1895	Blackburn Rovers *v.* Burnley	1-0	Division One
18 Apr 1896	Burnley *v.* Blackburn Rovers	6-0	Division One
03 Oct 1896	Blackburn Rovers *v.* Burnley	3-2	Division One
07 Nov 1896	Burnley *v.* Blackburn Rovers	0-1	Division One
26 Nov 1898	Burnley *v.* Blackburn Rovers	2-0	Division One
26 Dec 1898	Blackburn Rovers *v.* Burnley	0-2	Division One
07 Oct 1899	Burnley *v.* Blackburn Rovers	1-0	Division One
01 Jan 1900	Blackburn Rovers *v.* Burnley	2-0	Division One
08 Mar 1913	Blackburn Rovers *v.* Burnley	0-1	FA Cup
08 Sep 1913	Burnley *v.* Blackburn Rovers	1-2	Division One
01 Jan 1914	Blackburn Rovers *v.* Burnley	0-0	Division One
28 Nov 1914	Blackburn Rovers *v.* Burnley	6-0	Division One
03 Apr 1915	Burnley *v.* Blackburn Rovers	3-2	Division One
13 Sep 1919	Blackburn Rovers *v.* Burnley	2-3	Division One
20 Sep 1919	Burnley *v.* Blackburn Rovers	3-1	Division One
15 Jan 1921	Burnley *v.* Blackburn Rovers	4-1	Division One
22 Jan 1921	Blackburn Rovers *v.* Burnley	1-3	Division One
04 Feb 1922	Blackburn Rovers *v.* Burnley	3-2	Division One
11 Feb 1922	Burnley *v.* Blackburn Rovers	1-2	Division One
21 Oct 1922	Burnley *v.* Blackburn Rovers	3-1	Division One
28 Oct 1922	Blackburn Rovers *v.* Burnley	2-1	Division One
03 Nov 1923	Blackburn Rovers *v.* Burnley	1-1	Division One
10 Nov 1923	Burnley *v.* Blackburn Rovers	1-2	Division One
13 Sep 1924	Burnley *v.* Blackburn Rovers	3-5	Division One
17 Jan 1925	Blackburn Rovers *v.* Burnley	0-3	Division One
31 Oct 1925	Burnley *v.* Blackburn Rovers	1-3	Division One
13 Mar 1926	Blackburn Rovers *v.* Burnley	6-3	Division One
16 Oct 1926	Blackburn Rovers *v.* Burnley	1-5	Division One
05 Mar 1927	Burnley *v.* Blackburn Rovers	3-1	Division One
27 Aug 1927	Blackburn Rovers *v.* Burnley	2-1	Division One
31 Dec 1927	Burnley *v.* Blackburn Rovers	3-1	Division One
20 Oct 1928	Burnlcy *v.* Blackburn Rovers	2 2	Division One
02 May 1929	Blackburn Rovers *v.* Burnley	1-1	Division One
09 Nov 1929	Blackburn Rovers *v.* Burnley	8-3	Division One
15 Mar 1930	Burnley *v.* Blackburn Rovers	3-2	Division One

24 Oct 1936	Burnley *v.* Blackburn Rovers	0-0	Division Two
27 Feb 1937	Blackburn Rovers *v.* Burnley	3-1	Division Two
11 Dec 1937	Blackburn Rovers *v.* Burnley	3-3	Division Two
23 Apr 1938	Burnley *v.* Blackburn Rovers	3-1	Division Two
15 Oct 1938	Burnley *v.* Blackburn Rovers	3-2	Division Two
18 Feb 1939	Blackburn Rovers *v.* Burnley	1-0	Division Two
18 Oct 1947	Blackburn Rovers *v.* Burnley	1-2	Division One
06 Mar 1948	Burnley *v.* Blackburn Rovers	0-0	Division One
08 Mar 1952	Blackburn Rovers *v.* Burnley	3-1	FA Cup
18 Oct 1958	Burnley *v* Blackburn Rovers	0-0	Division One
28 Jan 1959	Blackburn Rovers *v.* Burnley	1-2	FA Cup
07 Mar 1959	Blackburn Rovers *v.* Burnley	4-1	Division One
17 Oct 1959	Blackburn Rovers *v.* Burnley	3-2	Division One
05 Mar 1960	Burnley *v.* Blackburn Rovers	1-0	Division One
12 Mar 1960	Burnley *v.* Blackburn Rovers	3-3	FA Cup
16 Mar 1960	Blackburn Rovers *v.* Burnley	2-0	FA Cup
08 Oct 1960	Blackburn Rovers *v.* Burnley	1-4	Division One
25 Feb 1961	Burnley *v.* Blackburn Rovers	1-1	Division One
24 Feb 1962	Blackburn Rovers *v.* Burnley	2-1	Division One
17 Apr 1962	Burnley *v.* Blackburn Rovers	0-1	Division One
06 Oct 1962	Blackburn Rovers *v.* Burnley	2-3	Division One
02 Apr 1963	Burnley *v.* Blackburn Rovers	1-0	Division One
01 Oct 1963	Burnley *v.* Blackburn Rovers	3-0	Division One
19 Oct 1963	Blackburn Rovers *v.* Burnley	1-2	Division One
10 Oct 1964	Burnley *v.* Blackburn Rovers	1-1	Division One
24 Feb 1965	Blackburn Rovers *v.* Burnley	1-4	Division One
09 Oct 1965	Burnley *v.* Blackburn Rovers	1-4	Division One
01 Jan 1966	Blackburn Rovers *v.* Burnley	0-2	Division One
27 Dec 1976	Blackburn Rovers *v.* Burnley	2-2	Division Two
08 Apr 1977	Burnley *v.* Blackburn Rovers	3-1	Division Two
26 Dec 1977	Burnley *v.* Blackburn Rovers	2-3	Division Two
27 Mar 1978	Blackburn Rovers *v.* Burnley	0-1	Division Two
26 Dec 1978	Burnley *v.* Blackburn Rovers	2-1	Division Two
14 Apr 1979	Blackburn Rovers *v.* Burnley	1-2	Division Two
27 Dec 1982	Burnley *v.* Blackburn Rovers	0-1	Division Two
04 Apr 1983	Blackburn Rovers *v.* Burnley	2-1	Division Two
17 Dec 2000	Burnley *v.* Blackburn Rovers	0-2	Division One

01 Apr 2001	Blackburn Rovers *v.* Burnley	5-0	Division One
20 Feb 2005	Burnley *v.* Blackburn Rovers	0-0	FA Cup
01 Mar 2005	Blackburn Rovers *v.* Burnley	2-1	FA Cup
18 Oct 2009	Blackburn Rovers *v.* Burnley	3-2	Premier League
28 Mar 2010	Burnley *v.* Blackburn Rovers	0-1	Premier League
02 Dec 2012	Burnley *v.* Blackburn Rovers	1-1	Championship
17 Mar 2013	Blackburn Rovers *v.* Burnley	1-1	Championship
14 Sep 2013	Burnley *v.* Blackburn Rovers	1-1	Championship
09 Mar 2014	Blackburn Rovers *v.* Burnley	1-2	Championship

ANGLO-SCOTTISH CUP

The Clarets took part in the Anglo-Scottish Cup on four of the five occasions the competition took place. The format was thus: sixteen English clubs competed in four groups of four, with the winners of each group qualifying for the quarter-finals. Clubs played each of the other teams in their group once, with two points awarded for a win, one for a draw, and a bonus point for each side that scored three or more goals in a single match.

Eight Scottish League clubs played a two-legged knockout round, with the aggregate winners of each tie qualifying to the overall quarter-finals. For the overall quarter-finals, each club was paired against a club from the other country, and the tournament then progressed in a knockout format, with each tie (including the final) being played over two legs.

Running from 1975 to 1981, the Clarets came on board in 1976, and the tournament became an enjoyable pre-season jaunt for the club, resulting in triumph in 1978/79.

1976/77

Blackburn Rovers, Blackpool, Bolton Wanderers, Bristol City, Burnley, Chelsea, Fulham, Hull City, Middlesbrough, Newcastle United,

Norwich City, Nottingham Forest, Notts County, Orient, Sheffield United, West Bromwich Albion, Aberdeen, Ayr United, Clydebank, Dundee United, Kilmarnock, Motherwell, Partick Thistle, Raith Rovers.

First Round
English Qualifiers

Group 1
Blackburn Rovers 1-1 Burnley
Bolton Wanderers 0-0 Blackpool
Blackburn Rovers 1-0 Blackpool
Bolton Wanderers 2-0 Blackburn Rovers
Blackpool 2-1 Burnley
Burnley 1-0 Bolton Wanderers

Pos		Pl	W	D	L	F	A	Pts
1	Bolton Wanderers	3	1	1	1	2	1	3
2	Blackpool	3	1	1	1	2	2	3
3	Burnley	3	1	1	1	3	3	3
4	Blackburn Rovers	3	1	1	1	2	3	3

1977/78

Birmingham City, Blackburn Rovers, Blackpool, Bolton Wanderers, Bristol City, Bristol Rovers, Burnley, Chelsea, Fulham, Hull City, Leyton Orient, Norwich City, Notts County, Oldham Athletic, Plymouth Argyle, Sheffield United, Alloa Athletic, Ayr United, Clydebank, Hibernian, Motherwell, Partick Thistle, Stirling Albion, St Mirren.

First Round
English Qualifiers
(NB Bonus points for scoring three goals)
Group 1
Burnley 2-1 Blackburn Rovers

Bolton Wanderers 1-0 Burnley
Blackburn Rovers 3-1 Blackpool
Burnley 0-4 -Blackpool
Blackburn Rovers 2-0 Bolton Wanderers
Blackpool 0-1 Bolton Wanderers

	Pl	W	D	L	F	A	BP	Pts
1 Blackburn Rovers	3	2	0	1	6	3	1	5
2 Bolton Wanderers	3	2	0	1	2	2	0	4
3 Blackpool	3	1	0	2	5	4	1	3
4 Burnley	3	1	0	2	2	6	0	2

Group 2
Bristol Rovers 1-0 Plymouth Argyle
Plymouth Argyle 1-1 Birmingham City
Bristol City 3-1 Bristol Rovers
Bristol Rovers 1-1 Birmingham City
Plymouth Argyle 0-2 Bristol City
Birmingham City 1-0 Bristol City

1978/79

Blackburn Rovers, Blackpool, Bolton Wanderers, Bristol City, Bristol
Rovers, Burnley, Cardiff City, Fulham, Leyton Orient, Mansfield
Town, Norwich City, Notts County, Oldham Athletic, Preston North
End, Sheffield United, Sunderland, Celtic, Clyde, Hearts, Morton,
Motherwell, Partick Thistle, Raith Rovers, St Mirren.

First Round
English Qualifiers
(NB Bonus points for scoring three goals)

Group 1
Preston North End 4-2 Blackpool
Burnley 3-2 Preston North End
Blackpool 0-1 Blackburn Rovers

Burnley 3-1 Blackpool
Blackburn Rovers 1-0 Preston North End
Blackburn Rovers 1-1 Burnley

	P	W	D	L	F	A	B	Pts
1 Burnley	3	2	1	0	7	4	2	7
2 Blackburn R	3	2	1	0	3	1	0	5
3 Preston N E	3	1	0	2	6	6	1	3
4 Blackpool	3	0	0	3	3	8	0	0

Quarter-finals

	Leg 1	Leg 2	Aggregate
Bristol City *v.* St Mirren	1-2	2-2	3-4
Burnley *v.* Celtic	1-0	2-1	3-1
Morton *v.* Oldham Athletic	3-0	0-4	3-4
Partick Thistle *v.* Mansfield Town	1-0	2-3	3-3 (2-4 on penalties)

Semi-finals

	Leg 1	Leg 2	Aggregate	
Oldham Athletic *v.* St Mirren	1-1	1-1	2-2	5-3 on penalties
Mansfield Town *v.* Burnley	1-2	1-0	2-2	3-4 on penalties

Final

Oldham Athletic 0-4 Burnley
Burnley 0-1 Oldham Athletic
(Burnley win 4-1 on aggregate)

1979/80

Birmingham City, Blackburn Rovers, Blackpool, Bolton Wanderers, Bristol City, Burnley, Bury, Cambridge United, Fulham, Mansfield Town, Notts County, Oldham Athletic, Plymouth Argyle, Preston North End, Sheffield United, Sunderland, Berwick Rangers, Dundee, Dunfermline Athletic, Hibernian, Kilmarnock, Morton, Partick Thistle, St Mirren.

First Round
English Qualifiers
(NB Bonus points for scoring three goals)

Group 1
Blackpool 2-2 Blackburn Rovers
Blackburn Rovers 2-2 Burnley
Preston North End 3-1 Blackpool
Blackburn Rover 1-1 Preston North End
Blackpool 3-2-Burnley
Burnley 1-2 Preston North End

	P	W	D	L	F	A	B	Pts
1 Preston North End	3	2	1	0	6	3	1	6
2 Blackpool	3	1	1	1	6	7	1	4
3 Blackburn Rovers	3	0	3	0	5	5	0	3
4 Burnley	3	0	1	2	5	7	0	1

1980/81

Blackburn Rovers, Blackpool, Bolton Wanderers, Bristol City, Burnley, Bury, Carlisle United, Chesterfield, Fulham, Grimsby Town, Hull City, Leyton Orient, Notts County, Oldham Athletic, Preston North End, Shrewsbury, Airdrieonians, East Stirlingshire, Falkirk, Hearts, Kilmarnock, Morton, Partick Thistle, Rangers.

Group 3
Bury 2-1 Burnley
Burnley 3-1 Oldham Athletic
Shrewsbury Town 3-0 Bury
Burnley 1-1 Shrewsbury Town
Bury 3-2 Oldham Athletic
Oldham Athletic 4-1-Shrewsbury Town

	Pl	W	D	L	F	A	B	Pts
1 Bury	3	2	0	1	5	6	1	5
2 Burnley	3	1	1	1	5	4	1	4
3 Shrewsbury Town	3	1	1	1	5	5	1	4
4 Oldham Athletic	3	1	0	2	7	7	1	3

MOST APPEARANCES

Competitive, professional matches only.

Name	Years	League	FAC	LC	Europe	Other	Total
1 Jerry Dawson	1907–29	522	46	—	—	1	569
2 Alan Stevenson	1972–83	438	33	36	—	36	543
3 John Angus	1955–72	439	45	25	10	2	521
4 Jimmy McIlroy	1950–63	439	50	3	4	1	497
4 Martin Dobson	1967–74,						
	1979–84	410	31	34	—	22	497
6 Jimmy Adamson	1950–64	426	52	3	4	1	486
7 Tommy Cummings	1947–63	434	38	6	0	1	479
8 Brian Miller	1955–66	379	50	13	12	1	455
9 Fred Barron	1898–11	400	23	—	—	—	423
10 Leighton James	1970–75,						
	1978–80,						
	1988-89	336	17	22	—	24	399

INTERNATIONAL CLARETS

Below is a list of every player to represent their country while with Burnley. By the end of the 2013/14 campaign some sixty-nine players had represented their country while at Turf Moor. Jimmy McIlroy is the Clarets' most-capped player with fifty-one appearances for Northern Ireland and he is also the top international goalscorer with ten goals.

Name	Nation	Pos.	Intl. Years	Caps	Goals
Aird, Jock	Scotland	DF	1954	4	0
Alexander, Graham	Scotland	MF	2007–2009	10	0
Angus, John	England	DF	1961	1	0
Bannister, Billy	England	DF	1901	1	0
Berisha, Besart	Albania	FW	2007–2009	10	1
Bikey, André	Cameroon	DF	2009–2010	4	0
Blacklaw, Adam	Scotland	GK	1963–1965	3	0
Bowsher, Stan	Wales	DF	1929	1	0
Boyle, Tommy	England	DF	1913	1	0
Bruton, Jack	England	MF	1928–1929	3	0
Caldwell, Steven	Scotland	DF	2009	1	0
Cassidy, Tommy	Northern Ireland	MF	1980–1982	4	0
Coates, Ralph	England	MF	1970–1971	2	0
Cochrane, Terry	Northern Ireland	MF	1978	4	0
Connelly, John	England	FW	1959–1963	10	4
Cort, Leon	Guyana	DF	2011	4	1
Coyne, Danny	Wales	GK	2005–2007	10	0
Cox, Ian	Trinidad & Tobago	DF	2001	4	0
Crabtree, Jimmy	England	DF	1894–1895	3	0
Dawson, Jerry	England	GK	1921–1922	2	0
Dobson, Martin	England	MF	1974	4	0
Duff, Michael	Northern Ireland	DF	2004–2012	21	0
Edgar, David	Canada	DF	2011–2014	23	1
Elder, Alex	Northern Ireland	DF	1960–1967	34	1
Elliott, Billy	England	MF	1952	5	3

Emerson, William	Ireland	MF	1922–1923	5	0
Flack, Hugh	Ireland	DF	1929	1	0
Fletcher, Steven	Scotland	FW	2009	3	0
Flynn, Brian	Wales	MF	1974–1984	34	3
Freeman, Bert	England	FW	1912	3	2
Gray, Phil	Northern Ireland	FW	2000	3	1
Guðjónsson, Joey	Iceland	MF	2007	4	0
Hamilton, Billy	Northern Ireland	FW	1980–1984	34	5
Harris, Gordon	England	MF	1966	1	0
Hill, Jack	England	DF	1925–1927	8	0
Hillman, Jack	England	GK	1899	1	0
Howieson, Cameron	New Zealand	MF	2012–2014	8	0
Hyde, Micah	Jamaica	MF	2004	4	1
Irvine, Willie	Northern Ireland	FW	1963–1968	17	6
Iwelumo, Chris	Scotland	FW	2010	2	0
James, Leighton	Wales	MF	1971–1978	23	3
Jones, Steve	Northern Ireland	FW	2006–2007	5	1
Kelly, Bob	England	FW	1920–1925	11	6
Lafferty, Daniel	Northern Ireland	DF	2012–2014	10	0
Lafferty, Kyle	Northern Ireland	FW	2006–2008	16	5
McCluggage, Andy	Ireland	DF	1927–1931	11	3
McDonald, Colin	England	GK	1958	8	0
McIlroy, Jimmy	Northern Ireland	MF	1951–1962	51	10
Michopoulos, Nikolaos	Greece	GK	2002	2	0
Miller, Brian	England	DF	1961	1	0
Morgan, Willie	Scotland	MF	1967	1	0
Morris, Billy	Wales	FW	1947–1952	5	0
Morrison, Tommy	Ireland	MF	1899–1902	4	1
Mosscrop, Eddie	England	MF	1914	2	0
Page, Louis	England	FW	1927	7	1
Papadopoulos, Dimitrios	Greece	FW	2002	1	0
Paterson, Martin	Northern Ireland	FW	2008–2013	13	1
Pilkington, Brian	England	MF	1954	1	0

Pointer, Ray	England	FW	1961	3	2
Richards, Dane	Jamaica	MF	2013	1	0
Taylor, Gareth	Wales	FW	2002–2003	4	0
Todd, Sammy	Northern Ireland	DF	1966–1970	8	0
Treacy, Keith	Republic of Ireland	MF	2011	1	0
Vokes, Sam	Wales	FW	2012–2014	10	2
Waterfield, George	England	DF	1927	1	0
Watson, Billy	England	DF	1913–1919	3	0
Willighan, Tom	Ireland	DF	1932–1933	2	0
Yates, John	England	MF	1889	1	3

OVERALL GOALSCORERS

Here are the men who have put the ball in the onion bag most often in Burnley history.

	Name	Years	League	FAC	LC	Europe	Other	Total
1	George Beel	1923–32	179	9	—	—	—	188
2	Ray Pointer	1957–65	118	12	2	0	0	132
3	Jimmy McIlroy	1950–63	116	13	1	1	0	131
4	Andy Lochhead	1960–68	101	12	9	6	—	128
5	Louis Page	1925–31	111	4	—	—	—	115
=	Bert Freeman	1911–21	103	12	—	—	—	115
7	John Connelly	1956–64	85	15	2	1	1	104
8	Jimmy Robson	1956–65	79	14	4	3	0	100
9	Bob Kelly	1913–25	88	9	—	—	0	97
10	Irvine	1960–68	78	9	8	2	—	97

GOALS, GOALS, GOALS – HOME

The Turf Moor records that both delighted and horrified the home support in almost equal measure:

Most home goals scored in one game (nine):
9 January 1892   Burnley   9-0   Darwen
28 March 1898   Burnley   9-3   Loughborough

Most goals scored by the opposition (seven):
3 November 1888   Burnley   1-7   Blackburn Rovers
5 April 2003   Burnley   4-7   Watford
26 April 2003   Burnley   2-7   Sheffield Wednesday

Highest winning margin (nine):
9 January 1892   Burnley   9-0   Darwen

Highest losing margin (six):
3 November 1888   Burnley   1-7   Blackburn Rovers
24 January 1987   Burnley   0-6   Hereford United
9 March 1999   Burnley   0-6   Manchester City

Highest aggregate (twelve):
28 March 1898   Burnley   9-3   Loughborough

MORE GOALS – AWAY RECORDS

The record goal hauls on the road, both scored and conceded:

Highest scoring win (seven):
10 April 1926   Birmingham City   1-7   Burnley
29 July 1928   Newcastle United   2-7   Burnley

Highest scoring loss (ten):

| 29 July 1925 | Aston Villa | 10-0 | Burnley |
| 19 January 1929 | Sheffield United | 10-0 | Burnley |

Highest winning margin (six):

| 10 April 1926 | Birmingham City | 1-7 | Burnley |

Highest losing margin (ten):

| 29 July 1925 | Aston Villa | 10-0 | Burnley |
| 19 January 1929 | Sheffield United | 10-0 | Burnley |

Highest aggregate (eleven):

24 October 1925	Manchester City	8-3	Burnley
9 November 1929	Blackburn Rovers	8-3	Burnley
29 October 2002	Grimsby Town	6-5	Burnley

Highest scoring draw (four):

8 November 1890	Aston Villa	4-4	Burnley
16 February 1907	Port Vale	4-4	Burnley
29 October 1932	West Ham United	4-4	Burnley
12 November 1955	Sunderland	4-4	Burnley
3 December 1960	Tottenham Hotspur	4-4	Burnley
2 November 1963	Stoke City	4-4	Burnley

CUP GOALS – HOME AND AWAY

These are the record scores (at both ends) in cup competitions for the Clarets.

Highest scoring win (nine):

10 February 1909	Burnley	9-0	Crystal Palace
26 January 1957	Burnley	9-0	New Brighton
17 November 1984	Burnley	9-0	Penrith

Highest scoring loss (eleven):

17 October 1885	Darwen Old Wanderers	11-0	Burnley

Highest winning margin (nine):

10 February 1909	Burnley	9-0	Crystal Palace
26 January 1957	Burnley	9-0	New Brighton
17 November 1984	Burnley	9-0	Penrith

Highest scoring draw (three):

23 October 1886	Astley Bridge	3-3	Burnley
6 January 1929	Burnley	3-3	Swindon Town
12 March 1960	Burnley	3-3	Blackburn Rovers
28 January 1961	Brighton and Hove	3-3	Burnley
29 November 1967	Burnley	3-3	Arsenal
15 September 1981	Burnley	3-3	Tranmere Rovers
30 July 1988	Rochdale	3-3	Burnley
15 November 1997	Rotherham United	3-3	Burnley

CLUB RECORDS

For reference whenever you need them, here are a list of club records that pretty much cover everything.

Youngest first team player in the league:
Tommy Lawton (sixteen years, 163 days) – against Doncaster Rovers, Football League Second Division, 28 March 1936.

Youngest first team player in Europe:
Alex Elder (nineteen years, 205 days) – against Reims, European Cup, 16 November 1960.

Oldest first team player in the league:
Jerry Dawson (forty years, 282 days) – against Liverpool, Football League First Division, 25 December 1928.

Oldest first-team player in Europe:
Jimmy Adamson (thirty-one years, 345 days) – against Hamburg, Football League First Division, 25 December 1928.

Most consecutive League appearances:
Jimmy Strong (203) – 31 August 1946 to 23 March 1951.

Most goals in a season in all competitions:
Bert Freeman (36) – 1912/13.

Most League goals in a season:
George Beel (35) – Division One, 1927/28.

Top League scorer with fewest goals in a season:
Eric Probert (5) –1970/71.

Most goals scored in a match:
Louis Page (6) – against Birmingham, 10 April 1926.

Goals in consecutive League matches:
Willie Irvine and Charlie Austin (7).

Most hat-tricks:
George Beel (10) – 17 November 1923 to 3 February 1931.

First international:
Jack Yates for England against Ireland – 2 March 1889.

Most international caps (total):
Brian Flynn for Wales (66 – thirty-four while with the club).

Most international caps as a Burnley player:
Jimmy McIlroy for Northern Ireland (51).

Most international goals (total):
Leighton James for Wales (10 – 3 while with the club) and Jimmy
McIlroy for Northern Ireland (10 while with the club).

Most international goals as a Burnley player:
Jimmy McIlroy for Northern Ireland (10).

BOXING CLEVER?

The Clarets have played eighty-two times on Boxing Day – that's a lot
of missed turkey leftovers – but history tells us that 26 December isn't
necessarily a profitable day for Burnley FC. Just twenty-five victories
is worse than one win in every three Boxing Day fixtures, and if you
add the seventeen draws, it means that the Clarets have failed to win
more than half the games played on this date. The total record is:
Played 82, Won 25, Drawn 17, Lost 40, For 102, Against 132.

Here are the opponents and season of our Boxing Day games – the
Clarets score is always first.

2013	Middlesbrough	A	0-1
2012	Derby County	H	2-0
2011	Doncaster R	H	3-0
2010	Barnsley	A	2-1
2009	Bolton W	H	1-1
2008	Barnsley	H	1-2
2007	Sheffield W	H	1-1
2006	Barnsley	A	0-1
2005	Stoke City	H	1-0
2003	Crewe Alex	A	1-3
2002	Wolves	H	2-1
2000	Barnsley	A	0-1
1999	Bury	A	2-4
1998	York City	A	3-3
1997	Chesterfield	H	0-0

1992	Brighton & HA	A	0-3
1991	Rotherham	H	1-2
1989	Carlisle	H	2-1
1988	Wrexham	H	1-3
1987	Rochdale	H	4-0
1986	Wrexham	A	2-2
1985	Tranmere R	A	1-2
1984	York City	A	0-4
1983	Bradford C	H	1-2
1980	Carlisle United	A	2-3
1979	Newcastle U	H	3-2
1978	Blackburn	H	2-1
1977	Blackburn	H	2-3
1975	Newcastle U	H	0-1
1974	Leeds United	A	2-2
1973	Liverpool	H	2-1
1972	Blackpool	A	2-1
1970	Blackpool	A	1-1
1969	Liverpool	H	1-5
1968	Liverpool	A	1-1
1967	Everton	A	0-2
1966	Stoke City	H	L 0-2
1964	Fulham	H	4-0
1963	Man Utd	H	6-1
1961	Sheffield W	H	4-0
1960	Everton	H	1-3
1959	Man Utd	A	2-1
1958	Leicester City	A	1-1
1957	Man City	A	1-4
1956	Preston N E	A	0-1
1955	Preston N E	H	1-2
1953	Preston N E	A	1-2
1952	Liverpool	A	1-1
1950	Everton	H	1-1
1949	Blackpool	H	0-0
1947	Preston N E	A	2-3
1946	Nottingham F	A	0-1

1938	Spurs	H	1-0
1936	Nottingham F	A	2-1
1935	Blackpool	A	0-2
1933	Oldham Ath	A	0-1
1932	Grimsby Town	A	2-1
1931	Preston N E	A	1-2
1930	Preston N E	A	0-2
1929	Bolton W	H	2-2
1928	Liverpool	A	0-8
1927	Leicester City	A	0-5
1925	Leeds United	H	6-3
1924	Huddersfield T	A	0-2
1923	Middlesbrough	A	0-3
1922	Aston Villa	A	1-3
1921	Man Utd	A	1-0
1919	Newcastle Utd	A	0-0
1914	West Brom A	A	0-3
1913	Sunderland	A	1-1
1910	Blackpool	H	1-1
1908	Derby County	A	0-1
1907	Stoke	A	0-0
1904	Grimsby T	H	1-0
1903	Stockport	H	2-0
1899	Stoke	A	0-3
1898	Blackburn	A	2-0
1896	Liverpool	H	4-1
1895	Small Heath	A	0-1
1894	Wolves	A	0-1
1893	The Wednesday	A	1-0
1891	West Brom A	A	0-1

CHRISTMAS CRACKERS?

By contrast with the Boxing Day fixtures, the Clarets record on Christmas Day is much healthier. The final match on 25 December was in 1957 – a 2-1 win over Manchester City – before players were allowed to spend at least a few hours with their families and maybe catch a re-run of *The Wizard of Oz*. It was 1913 before Burnley were beaten on Christmas Day, with no defeats in the first ten games played and only seven losses in thirty-eight games. It is historically the club's favourite day of the year. The complete record is: Played 38, Won 22, Drawn 9, Lost 7, Scored 77, Conceded 44.

1957	DIV1	Manchester City	H	W 2-1
1956	DIV1	Preston North End	H	D 2-2
1954	DIV1	Preston North End	H	D 2-2
1953	DIV1	Preston North End	H	W 2-1
1952	DIV1	Liverpool	H	W 2-0
1951	DIV1	Preston North End	H	L 0-2
1950	DIV1	Everton	A	L 0-1
1948	DIV1	Stoke City	H	L 1-3
1947	DIV1	Preston North End	H	W 1-0
1946	DIV2	Nottingham Forest	H	W 3-0
1937	DIV2	Fulham	H	W 1-0
1936	DIV2	Doncaster Rovers	H	W 3-0
1935	DIV2	Blackpool	H	W 3-2
1934	DIV2	Bolton Wanderers	H	W 2-1
1933	DIV2	Oldham Athletic	H	L 0-1
1931	DIV2	Preston North End	H	D 2-2
1930	DIV2	Preston North End	H	W 1-0
1929	DIV1	Bolton Wanderers	A	D 1-1
1928	DIV1	Liverpool	H	W 3-2
1926	DIV1	Liverpool	H	W 1-0
1925	DIV1	Leeds United	A	D 2-2
1924	DIV1	Huddersfield Town	H	L 1-5
1923	DIV1	Middlesbrough	H	D 0-0

1922	DIV1	Aston Villa	H	D 1-1
1920	DIV1	Sheffield United	H	W 6-0
1919	DIV1	Middlesbrough	H	W 5-3
1914	DIV1	West Brom A	H	L 0-2
1913	DIV1	Sunderland	H	L 0-1
1912	DIV2	Blackpool	H	W 4-0
1911	DIV2	Blackpool	H	D 1-1
1909	DIV2	Blackpool	H	W 5-1
1908	DIV2	Blackpool	H	D 1-1
1907	DIV2	Blackpool	H	W 2-1
1906	DIV2	Blackpool	H	W 2-1
1905	DIV2	Blackpool	H	W 4-1
1903	DIV2	Burton United	H	W 2-1
1900	DIV2	Gainsborough T	H	W 2-1
1893	DIV1	Sheffield United	H	W 4-1

HAT-TRICK HEROES

Here are the men who walked home with the match-ball having achieved a treble.

Date	Player	Goals	Opponents	Venue	Score	Comp.
15 Sep 1888	William Tate	3	Bolton Wanderers	A	4-3	FL
1 Mar 1890	Claude Lambie	3	Bolton Wanderers	H	7-0	FL
8 Nov 1890	Claude Lambie	3	Aston Villa	A	4-4	FL
15 Nov 1890	Claude Lambie	4	Derby County	H	6-1	FL
24 Jan 1891	Claude Lambie	3	Derby County	A	4-2	FL
7 Mar 1891	Tom Nicol	3	PNE	H	6-2	FL
9 Jan 1892	Tom Nicol	3	Darwen	H	9-0	FL
9 Jan 1892	Alex McLardie	3	Darwen	H	9-0	FL
1 Jan 1896	James Hill	3	Bury	A	4-3	D1
13 Apr 1896	Tom Nicol	3	Blackburn Rovers	H	6-0	D1

28 Mar 1898	Jimmy Ross	5	Loughborough T	H	9-0	D2
21 Apr 1898	Wilf Toman	3	Blackburn Rovers	A	6-0	TM
3 Dec 1898	Jimmy Ross	4	Sheffield W	H	5-0	D1
29 Dec 1899	Edgar Chadwick	3	Glossop	H	3-1	D1
28 Dec 1901	Matt Brunton	3	Doncaster Rovers	H	7-0	D2
31 Oct 1903	Dave Walders	3	Keswick	A	8-0	FA
31 Oct 1903	Billy Jackson	4	Keswick	A	8-0	FA
25 Feb 1905	Dick Smith	3	Port Vale	H	5-0	D2
15 Feb 1908	Dick Smith	3	Barnsley	H	4-1	D2
22 Feb 1908	Dick Smith	3	Chesterfield	A	4-2	D2
3 Oct 1908	Dick Smith	4	Gainsborough T	H	5-2	D2
16 Jan 1909	Arthur Ogden	3	Bristol Rovers	H	4-1	FA
10 Feb 1909	Dick Smith	3	Crystal Palace	H	9-0	FA
13 Nov 1909	Walter Abbott	3	Wolverhampton W	H	4-2	D2
25 Dec 1909	Ben Green	3	Blackpool	H	5-1	D2
28 Oct 1911	Bert Freeman	3	Fulham	A	4-3	D2
30 Dec 1911	Bert Freeman	3	Glossop	H	4-0	D2
20 Jan 1912	Dick Lindley	3	Hull City	H	5-1	D2
2 Mar 1912	Bert Freeman	3	Fulham	H	5-1	D2
14 Dec 1912	Bert Freeman	4	Leicester Fosse	H	5-1	D2
4 Jan 1913	Dick Lindley	3	Clapton Orient	H	5-0	D2
27 Sep 1913	Teddy Hodgson	3	Chelsea	H	6-1	D1
31 Jan 1914	Teddy Hodgson	3	Derby County	H	3-2	FA
11 Apr 1914	Bert Freeman	3	Derby County	H	5-1	D1
13 Jan 1920	Joe Lindsay	3	Thorneycrofts	H	5-0	FA
17 Apr 1920	Joe Anderson	3	Everton	H	5-0	D1
27 Nov 1920	Bob Kelly	4	Oldham Athletic	H	7-1	D1
25 Dec 1920	Joe Anderson	4	Sheffield United	H	6-0	D1
8 Jan 1921	Joe Anderson	4	Leicester City	A	7-3	FA
5 Feb 1921	Joe Anderson	5	Aston Villa	H	7-1	D1
24 Dec 1921	Bob Kelly	3	Middlesbrough	H	3-1	D1
8 Apr 1922	G. Richardson	3	West Bromwich A	H	4-2	D1
4 Nov 1922	Benny Cross	3	Nottingham Forest	H	8-2	D1
17 Nov 1923	George Beel	3	West Ham United	H	5-1	D1
29 Nov 1924	Tom Roberts	3	Bury	H	4-0	D1
5 Sep 1925	Tom Roberts	3	Leicester City	H	4-0	D1
26 Dec 1925	Louis Page	3	Leeds United	H	6-3	D1

10 Apr 1926	Louis Page	6	Birmingham City	A	7-1	D1
1 Sep 1926	George Beel	3	Newcastle United	A	7-1	D1
11 Sep 1926	George Beel	3	Bolton Wanderers	H	4-3	D1
20 Nov 1926	George Beel	3	Tottenham H	H	5-0	D1
1 Oct 1927	George Beel	3	Derby County	H	4-2	D1
21 Jan 1928	George Beel	3	Sheffield United	H	5-3	D1
29 Aug 1928	George Beel	3	Newcastle United	A	7-2	D1
24 Nov 1928	George Beel	3	Birmingham City	A	6-3	D1
1 Dec 1928	George Beel	3	Portsmouth	H	4-1	D1
23 Feb 1929	George Beel	3	Leeds United	H	5-0	D1
12 Apr 1930	Louis Page	3	Liverpool	H	4-1	D1
26 Apr 1930	Joe Mantle	3	Derby County	H	6-2	D1
3 Feb 1931	George Beel	3	Wolverhampton W	H	4-2	D2
29 Oct 1932	Tom Jones	4	West Ham United	A	4-4	D2
11 Mar 1933	Cecil Smith	3	West Ham United	H	4-0	D2
9 Dec 1933	Harry O'Grady	3	Lincoln City	H	3-1	D2
3 Nov 1934	George Brown	3	Hull City	A	3-1	D2
18 Jan 1936	Cecil Smith	3	Barnsley	H	3-0	D2
10 Oct 1936	Tommy Lawton	3	Tottenham H	H	3-1	D2
20 Nov 1937	Jimmy Stein	3	Southampton	H	4-0	D2
26 Nov 1938	James Clayton	3	Tranmere Rovers	H	3-1	D2
28 Dec 1946	Billy Morris	3	Coventry City	A	3-0	D2
11 Feb 1947	Ray Harrison	3	Luton Town	H	3-0	FA
20 Dec 1947	Jack Billingham	3	Portsmouth	H	3-2	D1
27 Nov 1948	Ray Harrison	3	Bolton Wanderers	H	3-0	D1
3 Dec 1949	Harry Potts	3	Everton	H	5-1	D1
8 Sep 1951	Billy Morris	4	West Brom A	H	6-1	D1
29 Dec 1951	Bill Holden	3	Middlesbrough	H	7-1	D1
3 Jan 1953	Les Shannon	3	West Brom A	H	5-0	D1
12 Feb 1953	Les Shannon	3	Tottenham H	H	3-2	D1
11 Apr 1953	Bill Holden	4	Sunderland	H	5-1	D1
7 Sep 1953	Billy Gray	3	Tottenham H	H	4-2	D1
17 Oct 1953	Bill Holden	3	Arsenal	A	5-2	D1
16 Jan 1954	Billy Gray	3	Middlesbrough	H	5-0	D1
5 Sep 1955	Peter McKay	3	Luton Town	H	3-1	D1
19 Nov 1955	Peter McKay	3	Portsmouth	H	3-0	D1
10 Mar 1956	Brian Pilkington	3	Chelsea	H	5-0	D1

5 Jan 1957	Ian Lawson	4	Chesterfield	H	7-0	FA
26 Jan 1957	Ian Lawson	3	New Brighton	H	9-0	FA
26 Jan 1957	Jimmy McIlroy	3	New Brighton	H	9-0	FA
9 Nov 1957	Jimmy McIlroy	3	Leicester City	H	7-3	D1
9 Nov 1957	A Cheesebrough	3	Leicester City	H	7-3	D1
21 Jan 1959	Jimmy Robson	3	Chelsea	A	3-1	D1
21 Nov 1959	Jimmy Robson	5	Nottingham F	H	8-0	D1
12 Dec 1959	John Connelly	3	Arsenal	A	4-2	D1
6 Sep 1960	Jimmy Robson	3	PNE	H	4-2	D1
1 Oct 1960	Jimmy Robson	3	Fulham	A	5-0	D1
22 Oct 1960	Jimmy Robson	3	Chelsea	A	6-2	D1
24 Oct 1960	Gordon Harris	3	Cardiff City	A	4-0	LC
17 Dec 1960	Ray Pointer	3	Arsenal	A	5-2	D1
16 Sep 1961	Ray Pointer	3	Birmingham City	A	6-2	D1
30 Sep 1961	John Connelly	3	Fulham	A	5-3	D1
22 Sep 1962	John Connelly	3	Manchester United	A	5-2	D1
14 May 1963	Willie Irvine	3	Birmingham City	H	3-1	D1
7 Sep 1963	Arthur Bellamy	3	Everton	A	4-3	D1
26 Dec 1963	Andy Lochhead	4	Manchester United	H	6-1	D1
12 Dec 1964	Andy Lochhead	3	Blackpool	A	4-2	D1
26 Dec 1964	Willie Irvine	3	Fulham	H	4-0	D1
24 Apr 1965	Andy Lochhead	5	Chelsea	H	6-2	D1
7 Sep 1965	Willie Irvine	3	Northampton T	H	4-1	D1
22 Sep 1965	Andy Lochhead	3	Doncaster Rovers	A	4-0	LC
11 Dec 1965	Willie Irvine	3	Fulham	A	5-2	D1
25 Jan 1966	Andy Lochhead	5	Bournemouth & B	H	7-0	FA
12 Feb 1966	Willie Irvine	3	Tottenham H	A	3-4	FA
26 Mar 1966	Willie Irvine	3	Nottingham Forest	H	4-1	D1
20 Aug 1966	Gordon Harris	3	Sheffield United	H	4-0	D1
25 Oct 1966	Andy Lochhead	3	Lausanne Sports	H	5-0	FC
26 Nov 1966	Andy Lochhead	4	Aston Villa	H	4-2	D1
21 Feb 1970	Steve Kindon	3	Nottingham Forest	H	5-0	D1
28 Sep 1971	Arthur Bellamy	3	Orient	H	6-1	D2
21 Oct 1972	Paul Fletcher	3	Cardiff City	H	3-0	D2
18 Sep 1973	Paul Fletcher	3	East Fife	H	7-0	TC
23 Nov 1974	Peter Noble	3	Newcastle United	H	4-1	D1
30 Aug 1975	Peter Noble	3	Middlesbrough	H	4-1	D1

Date	Player		Opponent		Score	
13 Sep 1975	Peter Noble	4	Norwich City	H	4-4	D1
18 Nov 1978	Peter Noble	3	Fulham	H	5-3	D2
27 Sep 1980	Steve Taylor	3	Millwall	H	5-0	D3
18 Jan 1982	Billy Hamilton	3	Altrincham	H	6-1	FA
7 Sep 1982	Billy Hamilton	3	Carlisle United	H	4-1	D2
1 Jan 1983	Steve Taylor	3	Sheffield W	H	4-1	D2
26 Feb 1983	Billy Hamilton	3	Charlton Athletic	H	7-1	D2
26 Feb 1983	Steve Taylor	3	Charlton Athletic	H	7-1	D2
3 Sep 1983	Billy Hamilton	3	Bournemouth	H	5-1	D3
26 Nov 1983	Kevin Reeves	3	Port Vale	H	7-1	D3
25 Feb 1984	Wayne Biggins	3	Lincoln City	H	4-0	D3
28 Apr 1984	Steve Daley	3	Port Vale	A	3-2	D3
17 Nov 1984	Kevin Hird	3	Penrith	A	9-0	FA
17 Nov 1984	Alan Taylor	3	Penrith	A	9-0	FA
2 Feb 1985	Kevin Hird	3	Rotherham United	H	7-0	D3
3 Sep 1991	Roger Eli	3	Chesterfield	H	3-0	D4
12 Oct 1991	G Lancashire	3	Wrexham	A	6-2	D4
18 Jan 1992	Mike Conroy	3	Gillingham	H	4-1	D4
4 Dec 1993	David Eyres	3	Rochdale	H	4-1	FA
4 Apr 1994	Tony Philliskirk	3	Barnet	H	5-0	D2
5 Oct 1996	Paul Barnes	5	Stockport County	H	5-2	D2
25 Feb 1997	Paul Barnes	3	Blackpool	A	3-1	D2
8 Mar 1997	Paul Barnes	3	Peterborough U	H	5-0	D2
3 May 1997	Andy Cooke	3	Watford	H	4-1	D2
31 Jan 1998	Andy Cooke	3	York City	H	7-2	D2
18 Sep 1999	Andy Payton	3	Colchester United	H	3-0	D2
28 Dec 1999	Andy Payton	3	Oxford United	H	3-2	D2
22 Aug 2000	Andy Payton	3	Hartlepool United	H	4-1	LC
5 Jan 2002	Ian Moore	3	Canvey Island	H	4-1	FA
5 Apr 2003	Gareth Taylor	3	Watford	H	4-7	D1
4 Oct 2003	Delroy Facey	3	Walsall	H	3-1	D1
5 Nov 2005	Ade Akinbiyi	3	Luton Town	A	3-2	Ch
12 Sep 2006	G Noel-Williams	3	Barnsley	H	4-2	Ch
12 Feb 2008	Andrew Cole	3	Queens Park R	A	4-2	Ch
11 Sep 2010	Chris Iwelumo	3	PNE	H	4-3	Ch
9 Aug 2011	Jay Rodriguez	4	Burton Albion	H	6-3	LC
31 Mar 2012	Charlie Austin	3	Portsmouth	A	5-1	Ch

| 15 Sep 2012 | Charlie Austin | 3 | Peterborough U | H | 5-2 | Ch |
| 2 Oct 2012 | Charlie Austin | 3 | Sheffield W | H | 3-3 | Ch |

HIGHEST CROWDS
INVOLVING BURNLEY

The biggest crowds on record at Turf Moor/neutral ground are as follows:

Pre-War (League):
50,000 *v.* Tottenham Hotspur, 26 March 1924.

Post-War (League):
52,869 *v.* Blackpool, 11 October 1947, Division One.

Pre-War FA Cup:
54,775 *v.* Huddersfield Town, 23 February 1924, FA Cup third round.

Post-War Cup:
52,850 *v.* Bradford City, 23 February 1960, FA Cup third round.

FA Cup Finals on neutral ground:
Liverpool 1913/14, The Crystal Palace, 72,778.
Charlton Athletic 1946/47, Wembley, 98,215.
Spurs, 1961/62, Wembley, 100,000.

Sherpa Van Trophy:
Wolves, Wembley, 80,841.

Play-Off Finals:
Stockport County, 1994, 44,806.
Sheffield United, 2009, 80,518.

HISTORIC GATES

Here's how many fans were watching the Clarets for particularly poignant seasons:

Average attendance for Burnley's first league season 1888/89: 4,200.

Average attendance for Burnley's Second Division Championship season 1897/98: 4,125.

Average attendance for Burnley's 1920/21 Championship season: 31,535.

Average attendance for 1946/47 Second Division Promotion and FA Cup finalist season: 25,856.

Average attendance for the 1959/60 Championship season: 26,978.

Average attendance for the 1972/73 Second Division Championship season: 14,083.

Average attendance for the 1981/82 Third Division Championship season: 6,936.